AF615660

Viennese Architecture 1860–1930 in Drawings

VIENNESE ARCHITECTURE 1860-1930 IN DRAWINGS

Edited by Karl and Eva Mang

Translation into English: Patricia Noris

Published in the United States of America
in 1979 by:

RIZZOLI INTERNATIONAL PUBLICATIONS, INC.
712 Fifth Avenue/New York 10019

Library of Congress Catalog Card Number: 79-64900
ISBN: 0-8478-0257-4

Printed in Germany

Foreword

While preparing the exhibition "Kommunaler Wohnbau in Wien 1923–1934" (Communal Housing in Vienna 1923–1934), we unexpectedly stumbled upon glass plate negatives from the Gerlach collection which show, in the charcoal technique typical of their period, designs by Peter Behrens, Karl Ehn, Rudolf Perco and others. Although the search for the original drawings remained unsuccessful, we did nevertheless manage to find sketches by Josef Hoffmann and Siegfried Theiß.

In view of the high quality of these drawings, even in comparison with the well-known graphic work of men like Joseph Maria Olbrich or Otto Wagner, we contemplated an exhibition of the original drawings of Viennese architects at the turn of the century which are to be found in Viennese museums and private collections. Unfortunately, it has so far not been possible to realize this project.

However, a proposal to put together a touring exhibition of photographs of the drawings aroused great interest at the cultural department of the Austrian Bundesministerium für Auswärtige Angelegenheiten. Ministerialrat Mag. Karl Kogler gave the project his full support. After a first stop in Rome, in the fall of 1978, the exhibition, "Austrian architecture 1860–1930, Sketches and Projects," will tour the world for the next several years.

Gerd Hatje, a good friend of ours for several years now, enthusiastically seized on the idea of publishing the drawings simultaneously in a book and thus rendering them accessible to a larger circle.

The works presented here, the first of which originated in the Ringstrasse era and the last in that of the working-class apartment houses in "red Vienna," will not only show the working method of renowned architects, but will serve as an example and stimulus for our own generation of architects, which is showing a growing interest in graphics.

We wish to thank all those who helped make the exhibition and the book a success. Foremost, in this context, we must mention the directors and the heads of the appropriate departments of the museums in Vienna, Berlin and Ljubljana as well as the private collectors; they not only placed the works but also their knowledge at our disposal.

In our office, Biella Fritzsche helped to review the extensive material, and Lotte Genetheim was untiring in the often difficult task of coordinating all activities. Dr. Peter Haiko of the Kunsthistorisches Institut der Universität Wien supplied us with important information. And finally, Professor Hans Mayr, Viktor Harrandt, Johanna Fiegl and Udo Otto, Vienna, Karl Heinz Paulmann, Berlin, and Miha Trasar, Ljubljana, greatly contributed to the success of the undertaking thanks to their photographic expertise.

Karl and Eva Mang

The sketches and drawings compiled in this book date from a time when modern architecture was on the long and difficult road leading from the first attempts of William Morris to adapt art and craft to the demands of a new age, to the International Style as it climaxed in the world-wide dissemination of the Bauhaus concepts. Characteristic of this period of transition is a sweeping polarization of positions, which range from rigid adherence to the procedures of the past to unconditional acceptance of the challenges of the industrial revolution.

The works were not only selected for their graphic quality; equally important was their significance in the development of Austrian architecture. However, since we made it a rule to include only extant original drawings and to exclude all prints or photos of drawings that cannot be traced, certain lapses could not be avoided.

After decades of the stagnation, caused by Metternich's conservative polices, in architecture as elsewhere, the work of developing the Ringstrasse area began shortly after 1857, under Emperor Franz Joseph I – the first activity of European dimension since the reconstruction of the town in the Baroque era. This project not only liberated Austrian talents, it also attracted a large number of gifted architects from all over Europe, among them Theophil von Hansen and Gottfried Semper. In contrast to the new order in Paris, where the façades of the new buildings had to comply with the rigid principles set down by Haussmann, the Ringstrasse architecture remained open to all styles, so that Historicism was able to take on its most pronounced form. Of all the Ringstrasse buildings, mainly palaces and residential houses (which individually are not always of the highest quality), the public buildings are most impressive: the Imperial Forum with the Hofmuseen, the Burgtheater, the Opera House, the University, the Town Hall. They greatly heightened the feeling for quality of the subsequent generation of architects and building artisans. This was due in no small measure to their graphic representation, which set a new standard in teaching as well as in practice. Many Ringstrasse architects passed on their knowledge and expertise in graphics directly: Theophil von Hansen, Eduard van der Nüll, August Sicard von Siccardsburg, Heinrich von Ferstel and Friedrich von Schmidt, all taught the next generation as professors at the Akademie or the Technische Hochschule. In any case, architectural drawing already had its tradition by then. First and foremost there was, from Vienna itself, Fischer von Erlach's *Entwurf einer historischen Architektur* (Draft of a Historical Architecture), published in 1721. Among other significant evidence of an existing tradition of architectural drawing was the splendid work in graphics being done at the Ecole des Beaux-Arts in Paris and by Karl Friedrich Schinkel, whose school Otto Wagner still attended.

The major figure of the period immediately following the Ringstrasse era was undoubtedly Otto Wagner, who is credited with taking the first step toward liberating architecture from Historicism. Wagner had very likely acquired the technical discipline and strict conception of graphic representation as the basis for the quality of his buildings during his apprenticeship at the Polytechnisches Institut and at the Berlin Bauakademie. The many preserved sketches and plans clearly reveal the working method of the foremost Viennese architect of the turn of the century: free-hand sketches, often hastily drawn on the back of old plans, were followed by pencil drawings in scale; from these, Wagner's assistants made the final plans with drawing ink on cardboard, finished with water colors or spray. Although Wagner's architectural development covered an astonishing amount of ground – from Historicism to Art Nouveau to Early Rationalism – his style of drawing changed very little during the course of his career.

Through his teaching at the Vienna Akademie, Wagner had a decisive influence on the subsequent generation of architects. It is amazing how strongly the style of drawing of the students of the "Wagner school" was influenced by their teacher – and how quickly it took on very personal characteristics in private practice. Wagner always managed to attract artists with above-average talents; one need only remember Joseph Maria Olbrich, Josef Hoffmann and Marcel Kammerer, who worked for a time in the atelier of the great pioneer of modern architecture in Vienna.

Side by side with the strict Wagnerian style of drawing, which retained some of its inflexible precision even during the Art Nouveau phase, flourished an almost Baroque delight in representation, vivid, exhuberant, a bridge between Historicism and Secession, and supported by the representatives of Late Historicism such as Ludwig Baumann and the willful, graphically highly gifted Friedrich Ohmann.

If the Akademie on Schillerplatz was, until about 1910, the crystallization point of architecture, the Technische Hochschule, which constantly brought forth great talents, played a decisive role in its further development, as did the Kunstgewerbeschule in the Stubenring, in large measure due to Josef Hoffmann, the cofounder of the Wiener Werkstätte.
The Wiener Werkstätte was noteworthy, among other things, for having at its disposal first-rate craftsmen who could execute a design from the barest sketch. This is clearly demonstrated in Hoffmann's furniture designs, where the conceptual and final working drawings are combined in a concentrated, astonishingly sparing form.
Adolf Loos, the great opponent of ornamentation, was no born draftsman. He is said to have destroyed nearly all of his drawings in 1922, before leaving for Paris. The sketches that survived are nothing more than hastily scribbled ideas; they show no trace of the brilliance of the Wagnerian drawing technique. In the case of Loos, a radiant personality and great eloquence were apparently sufficiently persuasive to win over his clients.
After World War I, art and architecture were confronted with a completely new situation. Large building projects for imperial Austria were now things of the past, and many eminent architects left the country, among them Josef Plečnik, Rudolf Schindler and Richard Neutra. However, even in early postwar years a new, important area of work opened up. This was the City of Vienna's social housing projects, whose preparation took place between 1919 and 1923, followed by a period of intense construction activity. Unfortunately, only the working plans of the huge projects (for example Karl Ehn's Karl-Marx-Hof) have as yet been found; of the perspectives, drawn in an Expressionistic charcoal technique, and well-known from photographs, there has so far been no trace.
With the reorganization and development of the workers' quarters as their principal task, the architects' field of activity had undergone a fundamental change compared to the preceding decades, or even to the entire past. What remained was the talent and the experience gained over generations as tools for recognizing and mastering new situations.

1
Theophil von Hansen
Herrenhaus. Aufriß der Hauptfassade. Tusche
Herrenhaus (Upper Chamber). Elevation of the main façade. Drawing ink

2
Theophil von Hansen
Herrenhaus. Aufriß der Hauptfassade. Bleistift und Aquarellfarbe
Herrenhaus. Elevation of the main façade. Pencil and water color

3
Theophil von Hansen
Herrenhaus. Schnitt. Schwarze und farbige Tusche
Herrenhaus. Section. Black and colored drawing ink

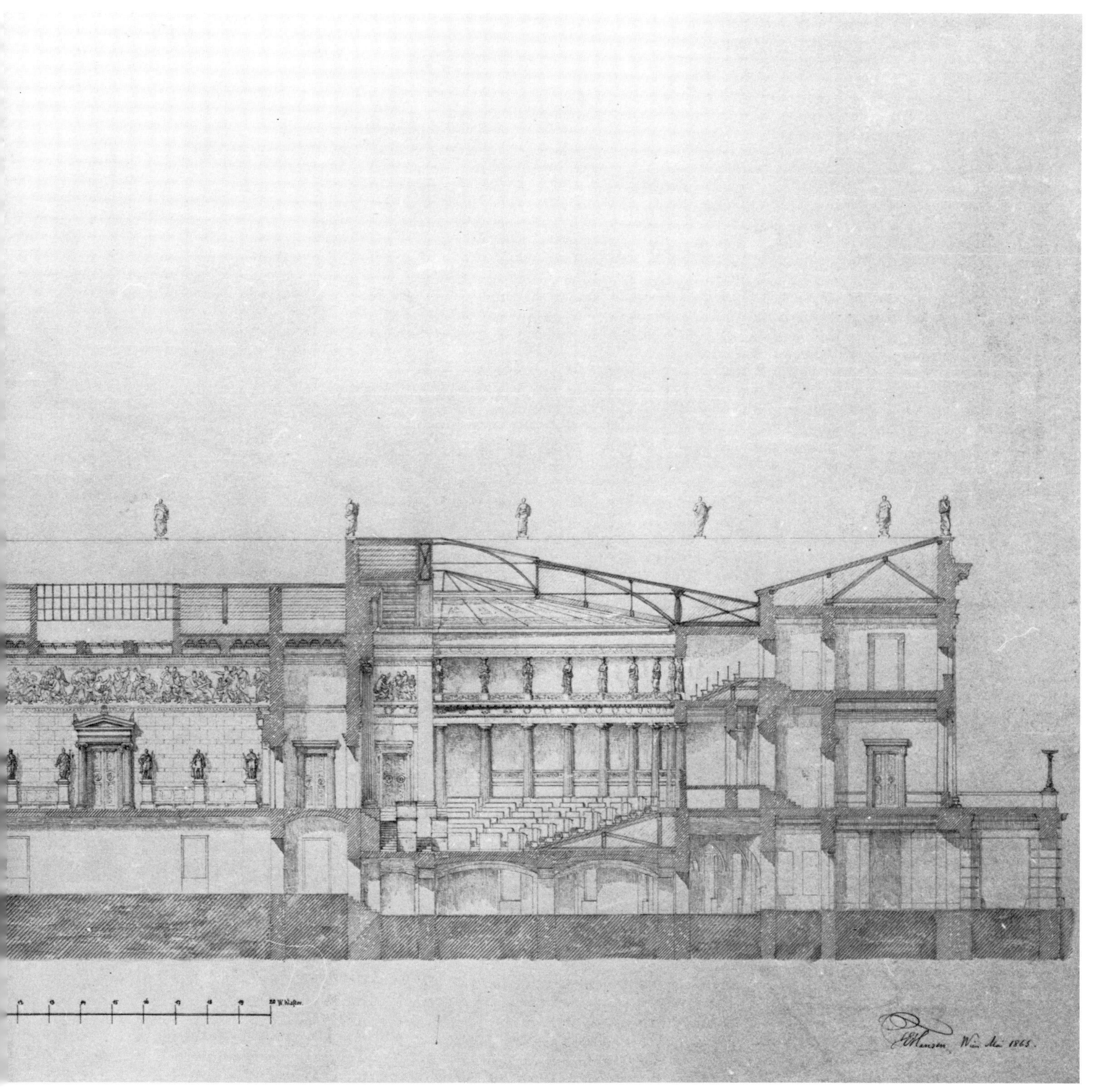
Hansen, Wien Mai 1865.

4
Theophil von Hansen
Parlament. Aufrißskizze der Seitenfassade. Tusche
Parliament. Elevation sketch of the lateral façade. Drawing ink

5
Theophil von Hansen
Parlament. Aufrißskizze der Hauptfassade. Tusche
Parliament. Elevation sketch of the main façade. Drawing ink

6
Theophil von Hansen
Parlament. Perspektivskizze. Bleistift und Kreide
Parliament. Perspective sketch. Pencil and chalk

7
Heinrich von Ferstel
Universität (1. Entwurf). Aufriß der Hauptfassade.
Tusche und Aquarellfarbe
University (first design). Elevation ot the main
façade. Drawing ink and water color

CADE
TRASSE.
1871

8
Heinrich von Ferstel
Universität. Aufrisse und Grundriß des Mittelrisalits. Bleistift
University. Elevations and plan of the projecting center. Pencil

9
Heinrich von Ferstel
Wohnhaus Wertheim, Schwarzenbergplatz. Aufriß der Hauptfassade. Tusche
Wertheim Residence, Schwarzenbergplatz. Elevation of the main façade. Drawing ink

10
Gottfried Semper/Carl von Hasenauer
Anlage zur Verbindung der Hofburg mit den Museen. Vogelperspektive. Schwarze und braune Tusche
Structure linking the Hofburg with the museums. Bird's-eye view. Black and brown drawing ink

11
Gottfried Semper/Carl von Hasenauer
Ausbau der Hofburg in Verbindung mit dem Neubau der Museen und dem Hofburgtheater. Aufriß und Schnitt. Tusche, braun laviert
Extension of the Hofburg in connection with the new construction of the museums and of the Hofburgtheater. Elevation and section. Drawing ink with brown wash

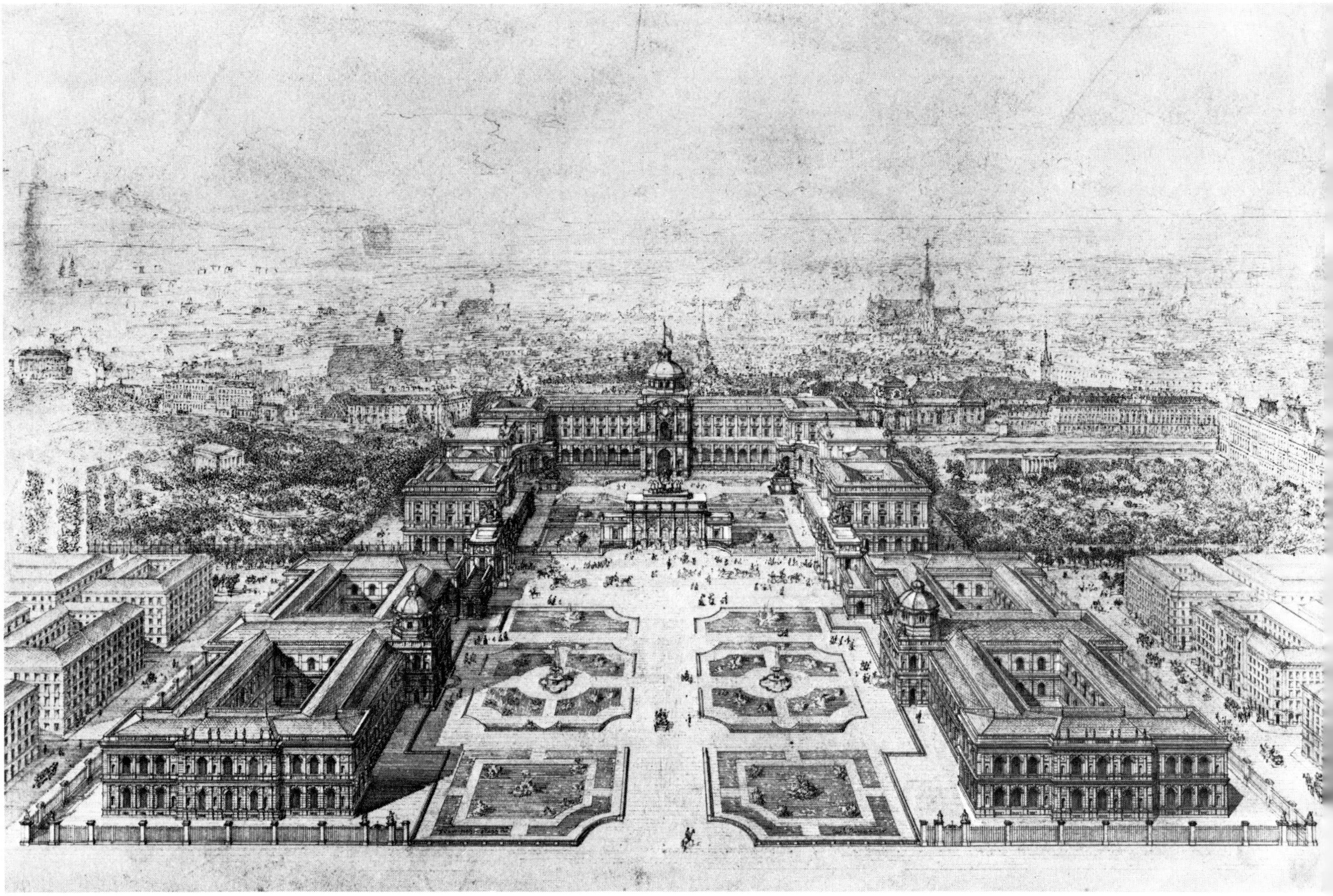

Architecture is a pure inventiv art, for it has no ready made prototypes in nature for its forms, they are free productions of human imagination and intellect. It would therefore, with respect to this, appear to be the freest among the different arts of design, if it was not entirely depending on the laws of nature in general and the mechanical laws of matter especially; for whatever object of architectural art we may consider, its first and original conception will have rosen from the necessity of providing for some material want, especially that of protection and shelter against injuries of clime and elements, or of other hostile powers; and as we can obtain protection of this kind only by solid combinations of matters, which nature procures, we necessarily are constrained for those constructions to the strict observance of the statical and mechanical principles.
This material dependency on natural laws and conditions which remains the same everwhere and at all times gives to the works of architecture a certain character of necessity and in a certain degree makes them appear to be nature works, but such which nature created through the medium of reasoning and free acting beings.

Gottfried Semper, 1854[1]

12
Gottfried Semper/Carl von Hasenauer
Hofschauspielhaus. Grundriß der Logenebene.
Tusche
Hofschauspielhaus. Plan of the box level. Drawing ink

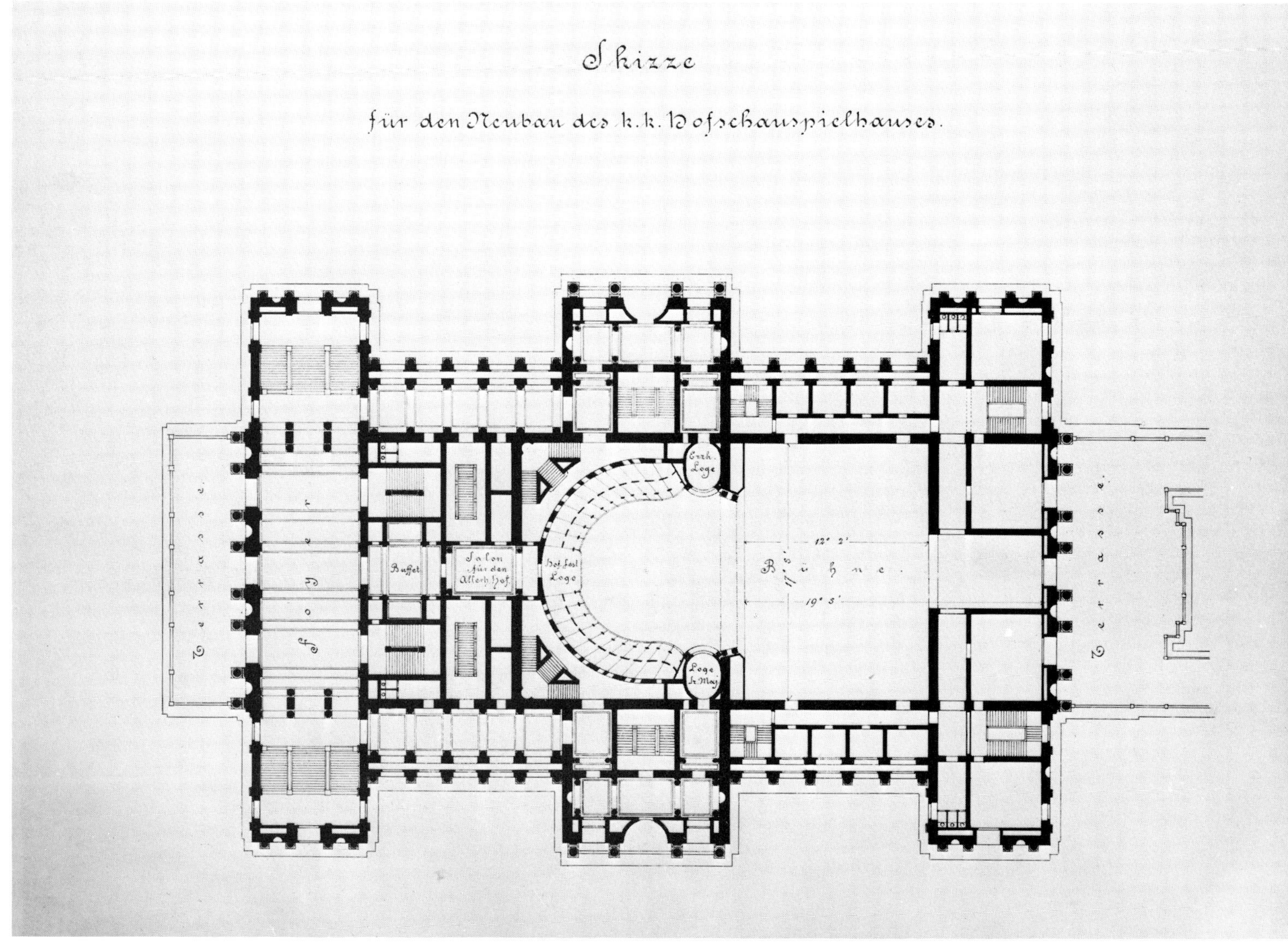

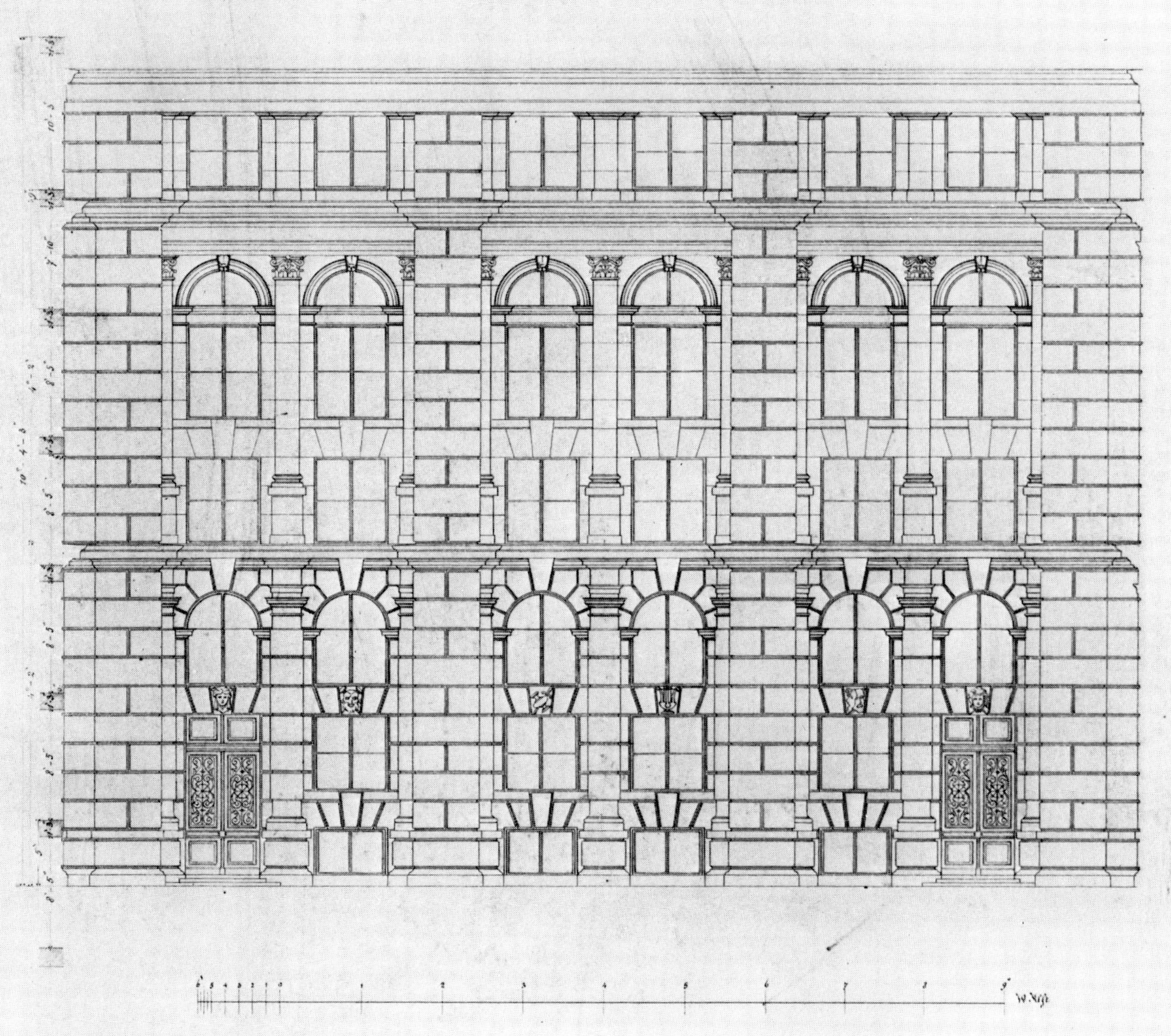

13
Gottfried Semper/Carl von Hasenauer
Hofschauspielhaus. Aufriß eines Teils der Seitenfassade. Tusche
Hofschauspielhaus. Elevation of a part of the lateral façade. Drawing ink

14
August Sicard von Siccardsburg/Eduard van der Nüll
Oper. Aufriß der Hauptfassade. Tusche
Opera. Elevation of the main façade. Drawing ink

BAU S.M. HOFBURG · PARTERRESAAL · 1:25 ·
WIEN, IM MÄRZ 1914

15
Ludwig Baumann
Rudolf-von-Habsburg-Denkmal. Perspektivskizze. Bleistift
Rudolf von Habsburg Monument. Perspective sketch. Pencil

16
Ludwig Baumann
Hofburg. Aufriß einer Wand im Parterresaal. Bleistift, Tusche und Aquarellfarbe
Hofburg. Elevation of a wall in the parterre hall. Pencil, drawing ink and water color

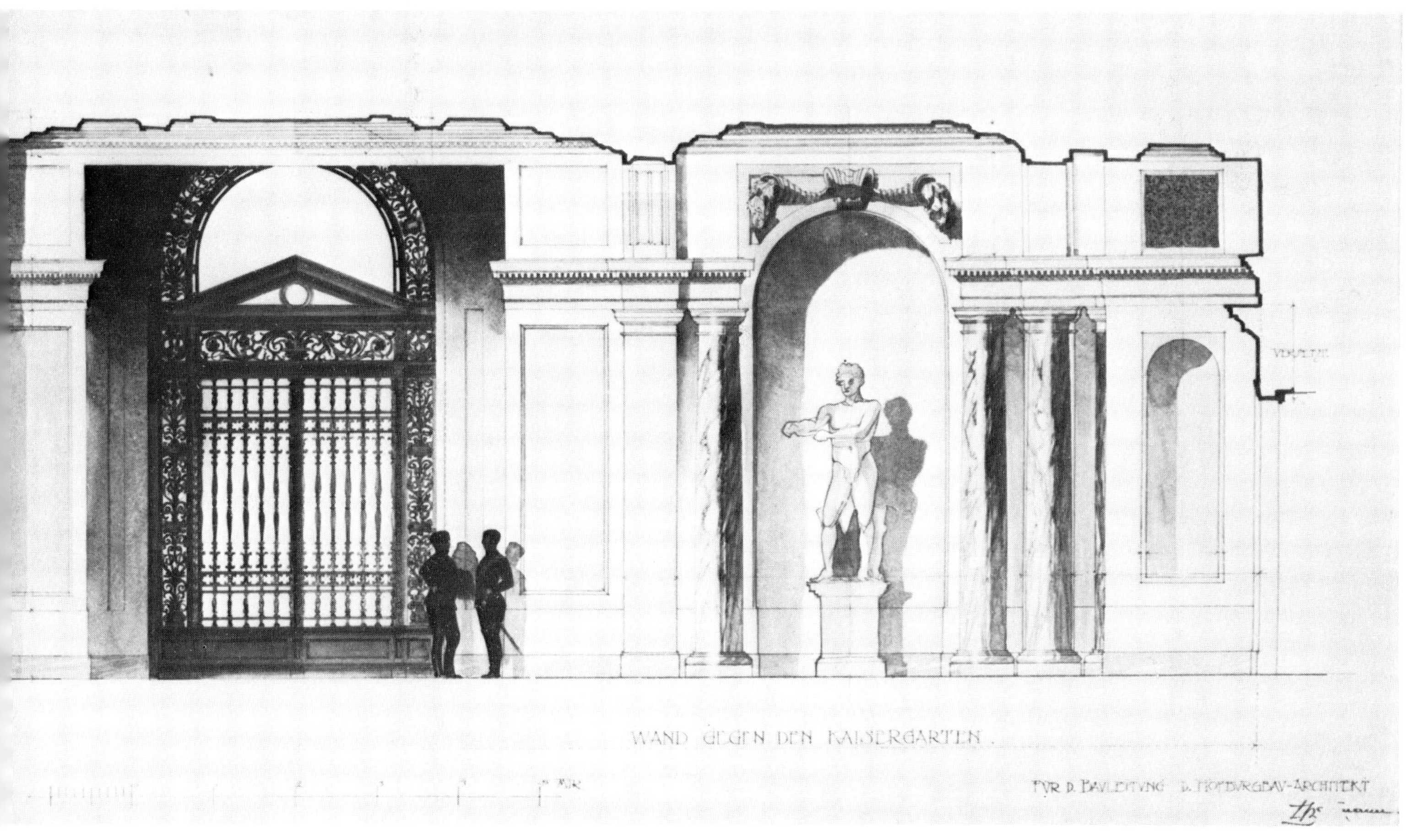

17
Friedrich Ohmann
Versicherungsgebäude in Prag. Perspektivskizze. Sepia, laviert
Insurance building in Prague. Perspective sketch. Sepia with wash

18
Friedrich Ohmann
Palmenhaus. Perspektivskizze. Tusche, laviert, Bleistift und Farbstift
Palm house. Perspective sketch. Drawing ink with wash, pencil and crayon

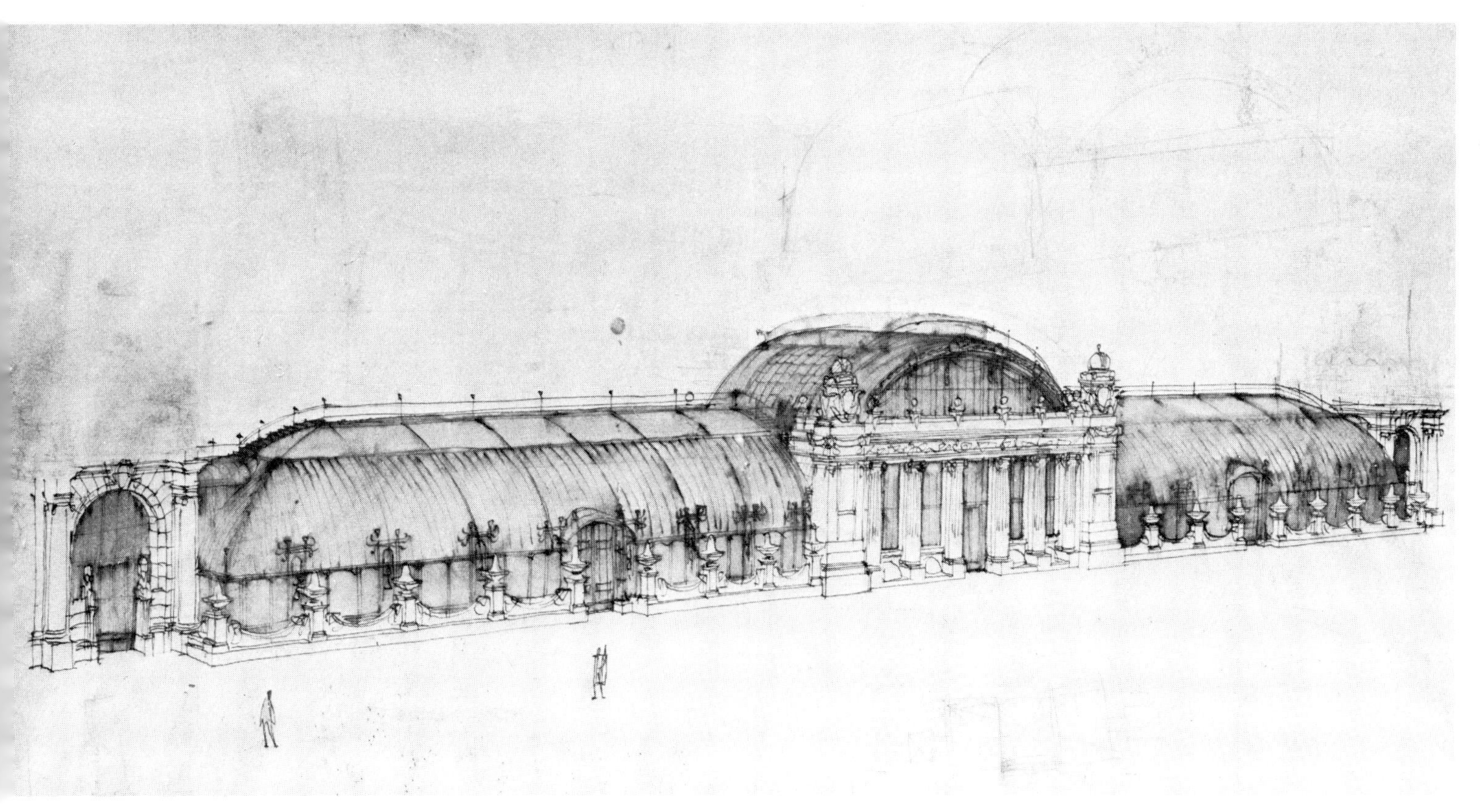

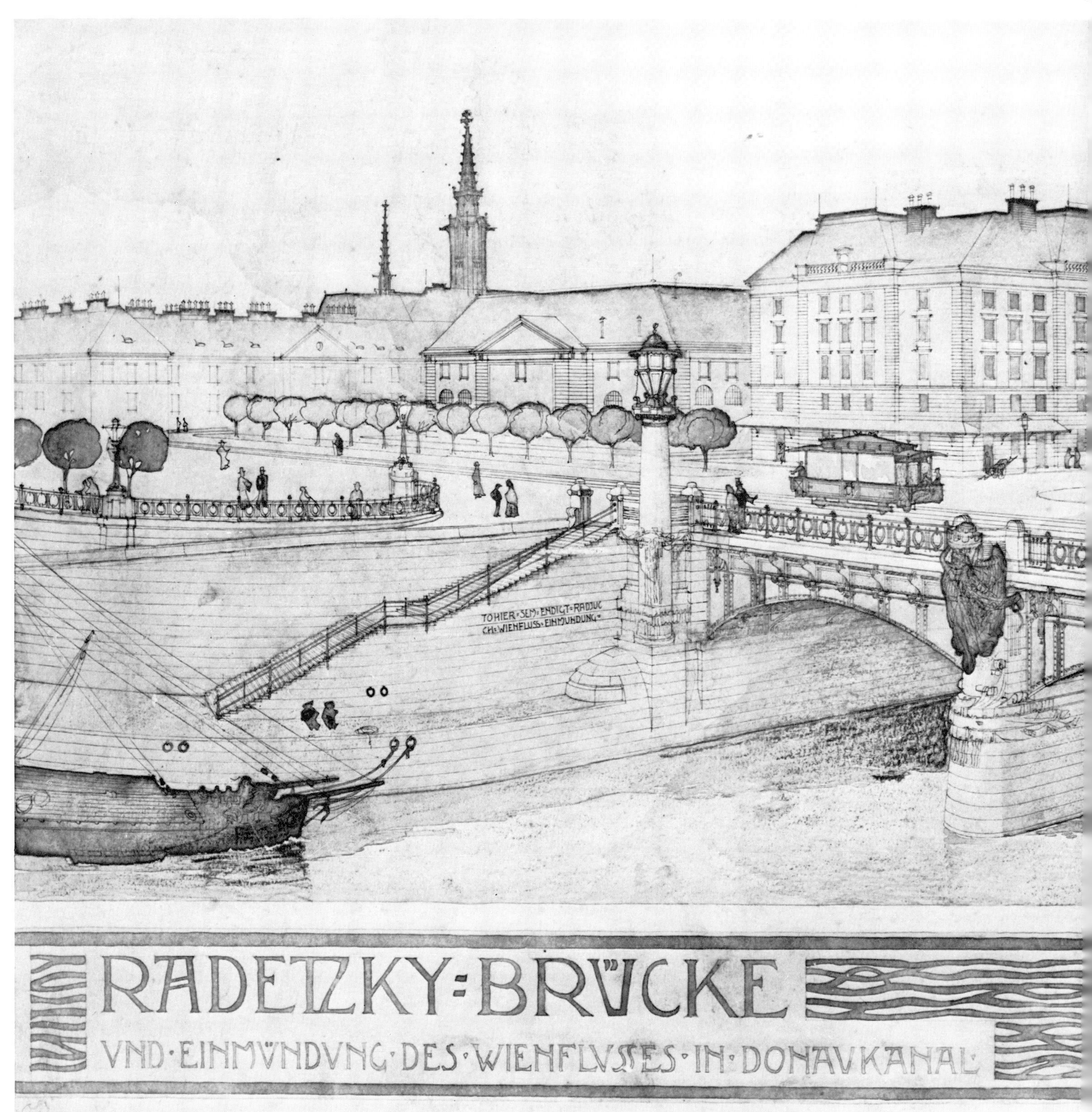
RADETZKY=BRÜCKE
UND·EINMÜNDUNG·DES·WIENFLUSSES·IN·DONAUKANAL·

19
Friedrich Ohmann
Radetzkybrücke. Perspektive. Tusche und Aquarellfarbe
Radetzkybrücke. Perspective. Drawing ink and water color

20
Friedrich Ohmann
Hofburg. Schnitt. Tusche, Bleistift und Farbstift
Hofburg. Section. Drawing ink, pencil and crayon

21
Friedrich Ohmann
Hofburg. Perspektivischer Schnitt durch die Stiege. Bleistift
Hofburg. Perspective section through the staircase. Pencil

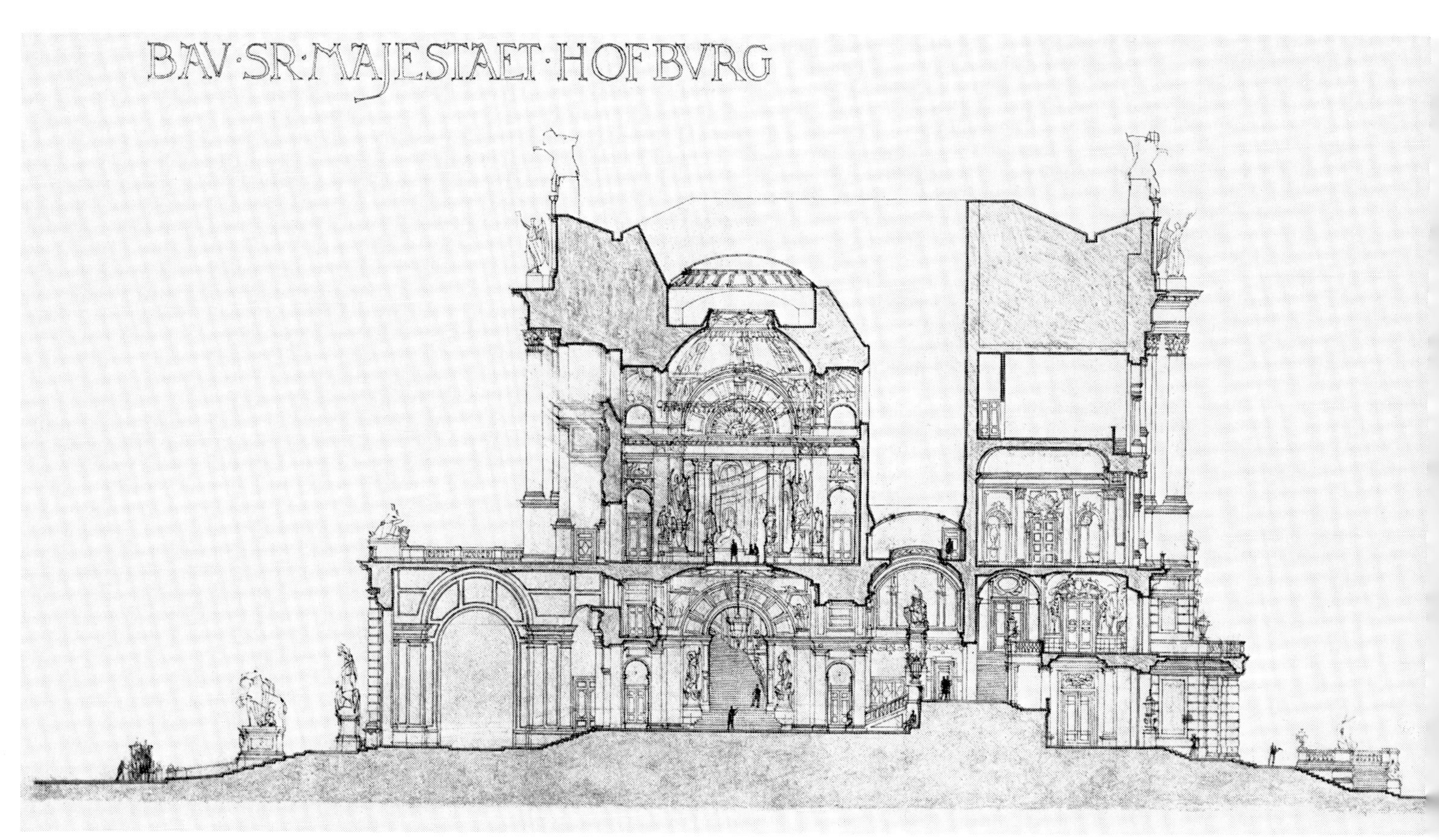

I STOCK
MEZZANIN
ZUM GARTEN
ZUM GARTEN
PARTERRE
ZUFAHRT

22
Friedrich Ohmann
Kaiserin-Elisabeth-Denkmal. Aufrißskizze der Bepflanzung. Tusche, Bleistift und Farbstift
Kaiserin Elisabeth Monument. Elevation sketch of the planting. Drawing ink, pencil and crayon

23
Friedrich Ohmann
Kaiserin-Elisabeth-Denkmal. Aufrißskizze. Tusche, Aquarellfarbe und Pastellkreide
Kaiserin Elisabeth Monument. Elevation sketch. Drawing ink, water color and pastel chalk

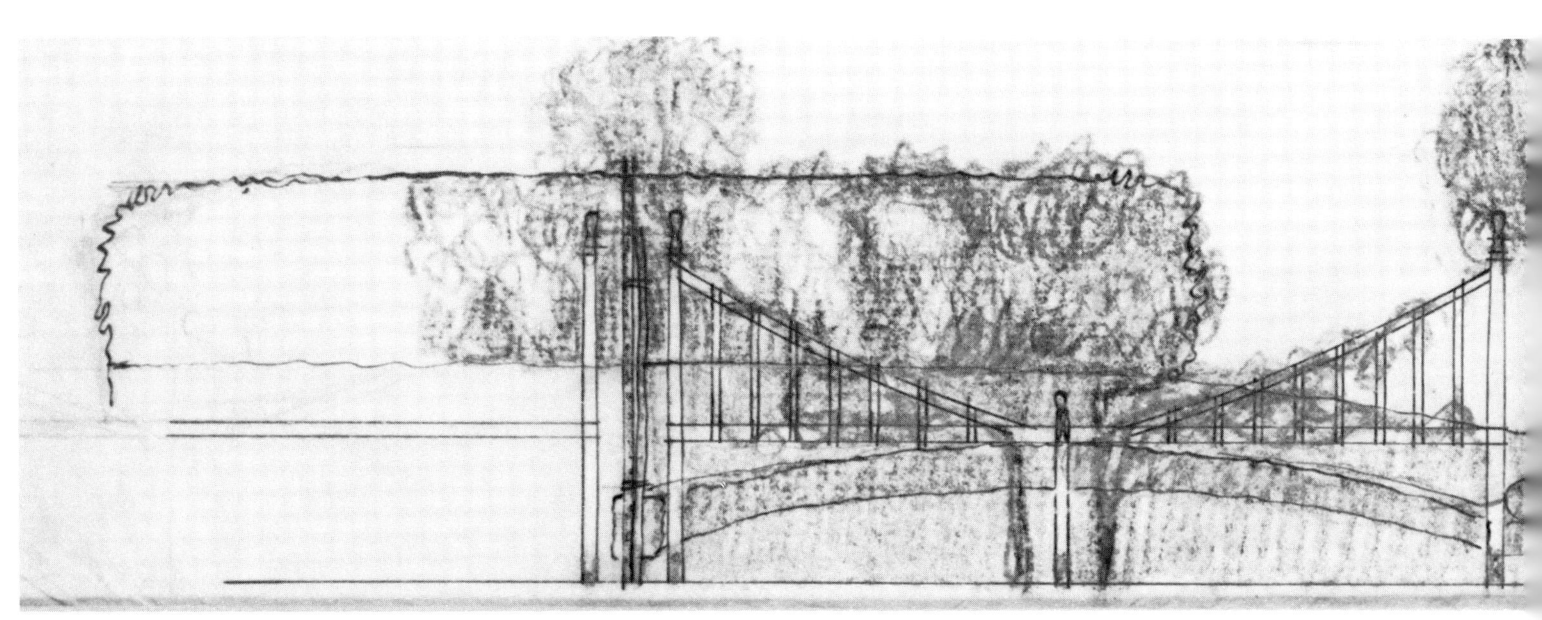

24
Friedrich Ohmann/Josef Hackhofer
Wienflußeinmündung im Stadtpark. Perspektive.
Tusche und Aquarellfarbe
Mouth of the Wienfluß in the Stadtpark. Perspective. Drawing ink and water color

25
Friedrich Ohmann
Dianabad. Perspektive. Tusche und Bleistift, weiß gehöht
Dianabad. Perspective. Drawing ink and pencil, heightened with white

26
Otto Wagner
Justizpalast. Aufriß der Seitenfassade. Tusche und Aquarellfarbe
Palace of Justice. Elevation of the lateral façade. Drawing ink and water color

27
Otto Wagner
Justizpalast. Schnitt. Tusche und Aquarellfarbe
Palace of Justice. Section. Drawing ink and water color

28
Otto Wagner
Kapuzinerkirche mit Kaisergruft (Umbaustudie). Perspektive. Tusche, laviert und weiß gehöht
Kapuzinerkirche with imperial tomb (reconstruction study). Perspective. Drawing ink with wash, heightened with white

29
Otto Wagner
Hofpavillon der Stadtbahnhaltestelle Hietzing. Aufriß. Tusche und Aquarellfarbe, weiß gehöht
Court Pavilion of the Hietzing city railway station. Elevation. Drawing ink and water color, heightened with white

30
Otto Wagner
Stadtbahnhaltestelle Karlsplatz. Perspektiven und Grundrißausschnitt. Tusche und Aquarellfarbe
Karlsplatz city railway station. Perspectives and ground plan detail. Drawing ink and water color

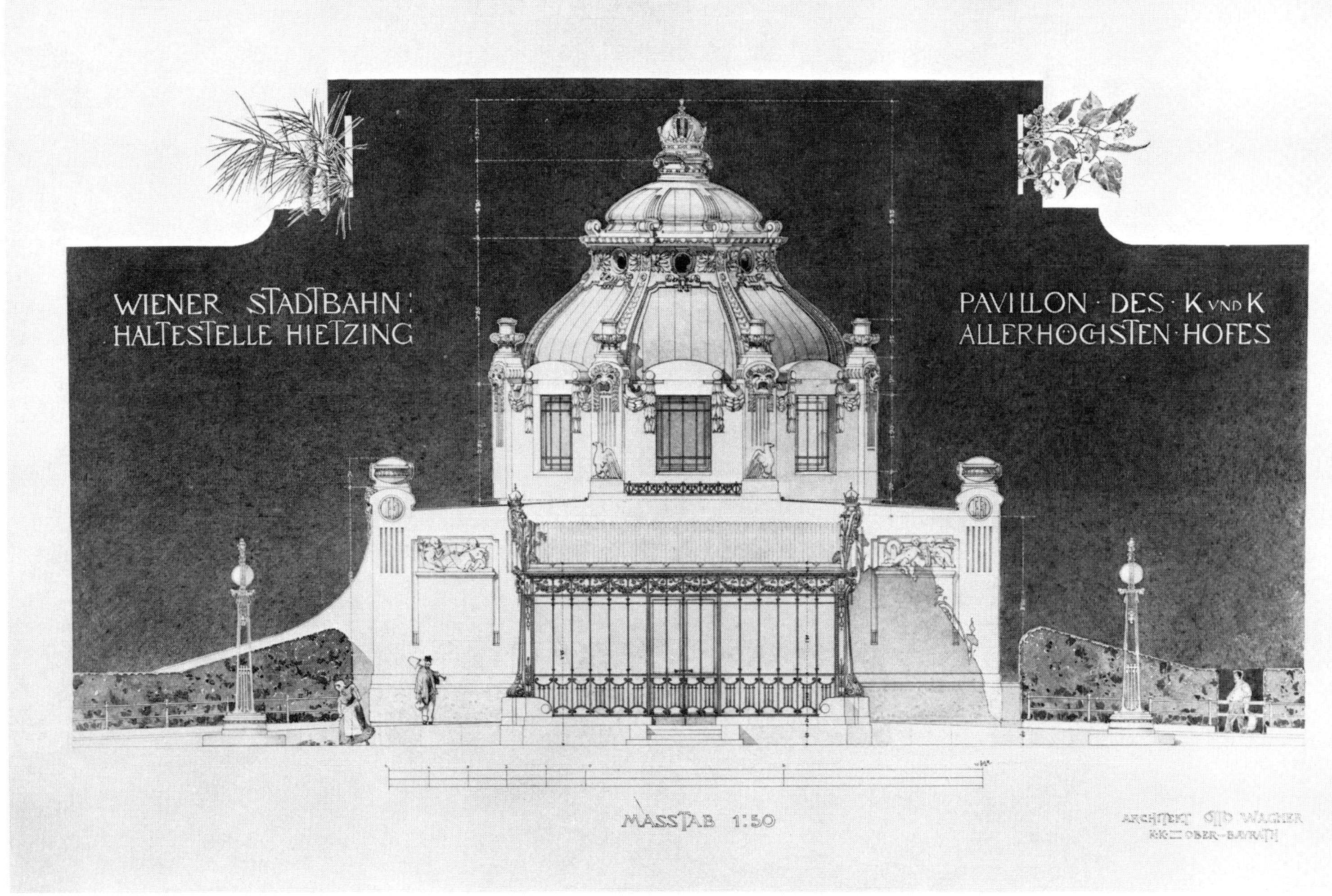

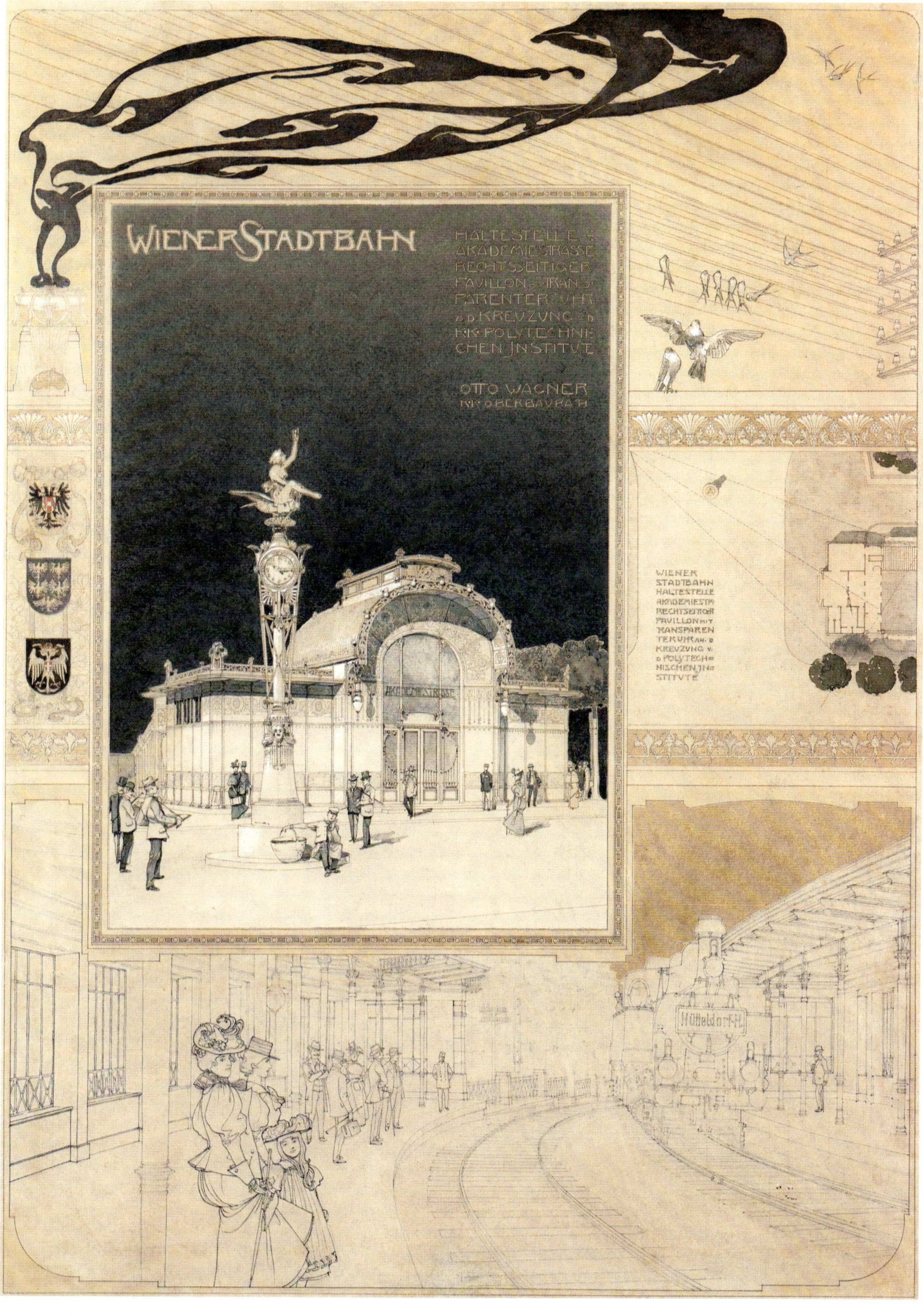

WIENER STADTBAHN
HALTESTELLE
AKADEMIESTRASSE
RECHTSSEITIGER
PAVILLON TRANS-
PARENTER UHR
A. D. KREUZUNG D.
K.K. POLYTECHNI-
CHEN INSTITUTE
OTTO WAGNER
K.K. OBERBAURATH
WIENER
STADTBAHN
HALTESTELLE
AKADEMIESTR.
RECHTSSEITIGER
PAVILLON MIT
TRANSPAREN
TER UHR AN D.
KREUZUNG V.
D. POLYTECH=
NISCHEN IN=
STITUTE
Hütteldorf-H.

31
Otto Wagner
Akademie der bildenden Künste. Vogelperspektive. Tusche und Aquarellfarbe, Schrift Gold gehöht
Akademie der bildenden Künste. Bird's-eye view. Drawing ink and water color, lettering heightened with gold

32
Otto Wagner
Kunstgalerie. Aufrißskizze der Hauptfassade. Bleistift und gelber Farbstift
Art gallery. Elevation sketch of the main façade. Pencil and yellow crayon

33
Otto Wagner
Galerie für Werke der Kunst unserer Zeit. Aufriß der Hauptfassade. Tusche und Aquarellfarbe
Galerie für Werke der Kunst unserer Zeit. Elevation of the main façade. Drawing ink and water color

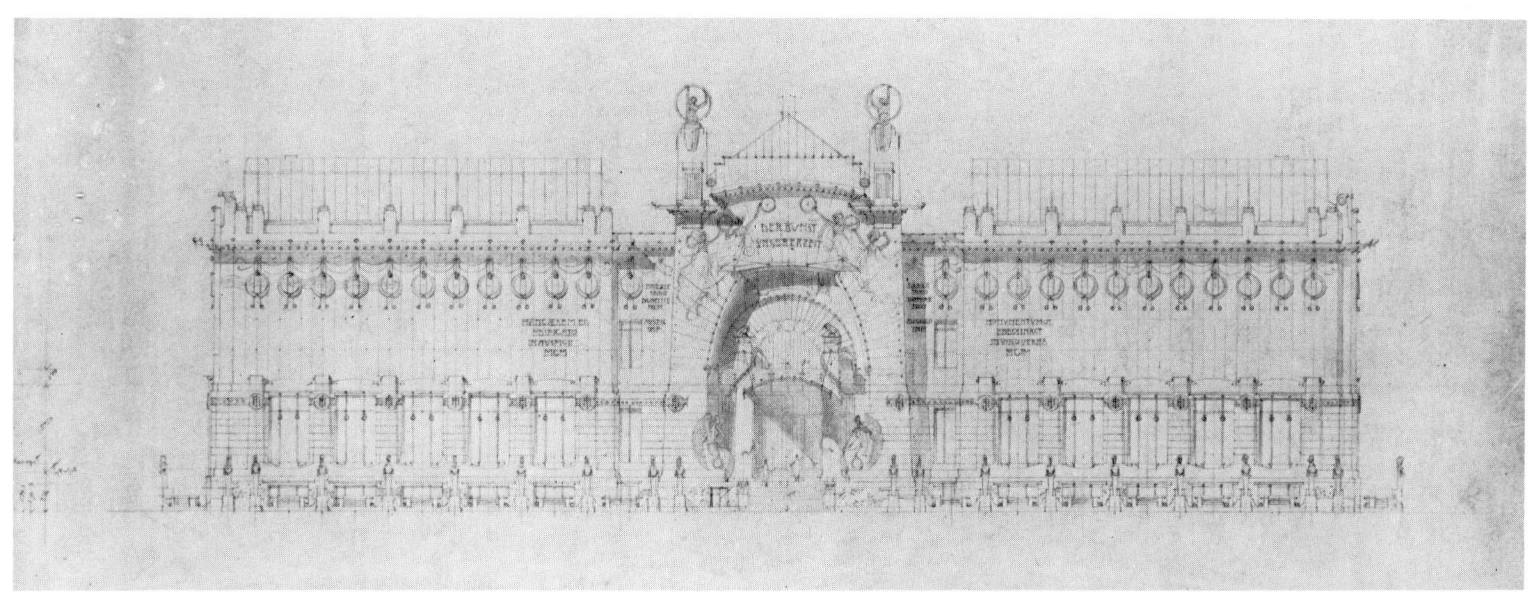

34
Otto Wagner
Kaiser-Franz-Joseph-Stadtmuseum (Projekt zum allgemeinen Wettbewerb). Perspektive. Tusche und Farbstift
Kaiser-Franz-Joseph-Stadtmuseum (project for the open competition). Perspective. Drawing ink and crayon

35
Otto Wagner
Internationale Kunstausstellung in Wien. Aufriß der Seitenfassade und Schnitt. Tusche und Aquarellfarbe
International art exhibition in Vienna. Elevation of the lateral façade and section. Drawing ink and water color

36
Otto Wagner
Internationale Kunstausstellung in Wien. Aufriß der Hauptfassade. Tusche und Aquarellfarbe
International art exhibition in Vienna. Elevation of the main façade. Drawing ink and water color

37
Otto Wagner
Internationale Kunstausstellung in Wien. Grundriß. Tusche und Aquarellfarbe
International art exhibition in Vienna. Ground plan. Drawing ink and water color

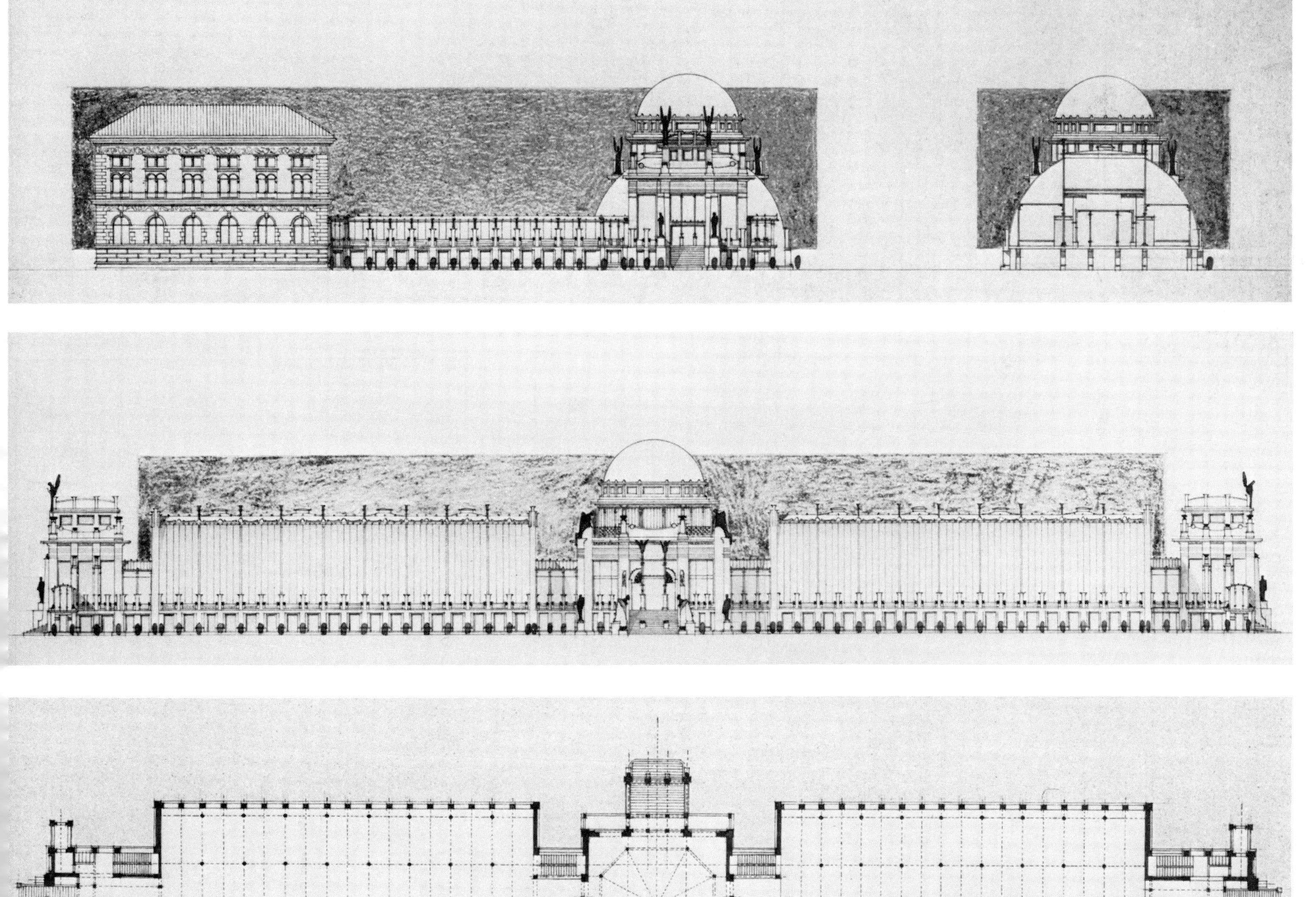

38
Otto Wagner
Postsparkassenamt. Aufriß der Hauptfassade. Tusche
Postal Savings Bank. Elevation of the main façade. Drawing ink

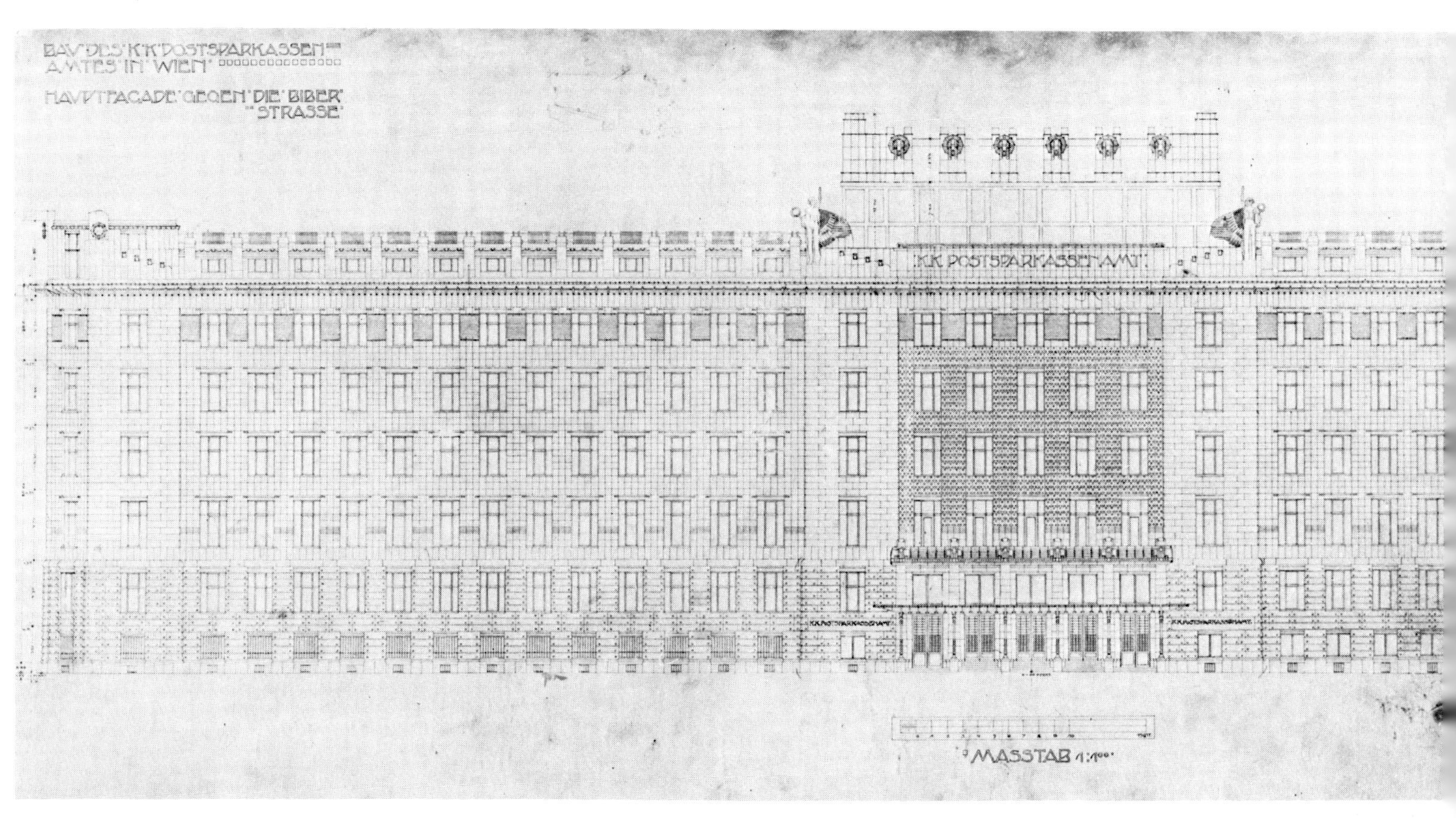

The major point of nearly all modern buildings is how successfully their external appearance manages to be an almost exact copy of a particular style of architecture. Good copies, for which, as a rule, much is sacrificed, are then termed examples of pure style and generally constitute the criterion by which a building is judged.

Certain styles of architecture are usurped for particular purposes, and the general public, and unfortunately many architects as well, are of the opinion that this – must be so.

At present, the situation has reached the point where building styles change like fashions and works of art have deliberately been made "old" to give them a pedigree dating from past centuries.

Thus are form and style truly misused, and, were the situation not quite so sad, it could be called the farce of architecture.

That this cannot possibly be right needs no further proof.

Let us, by way of contrast, take a look at the works of art of previous centuries.

From antiquity to the Renaissance, even up to the Empire style of our century – the work of art was always a reflection of its time.

And here lies the secret. Art and artists should and must represent their times. The salvation of the future cannot lie in whipping through all styles of architecture, as has happened in the past few decades. We are all capable of utilizing and developing inherited forms with skill and taste, whether they support, tower, crown, or show us how to structure a space. But the starting point of every artistic endeavor must be the necessity, the ability, the methods and the characteristics of "our" era.

"Artis sola domina necessitas".

(Art knows only one master – necessity.)

Therefore, when you set about solving a task, always ask: how will it suit the contemporaries, the contract, the genius loci, the climate, the available materials, the pecuniary means? Only thus can you hope to evoke true appreciation, and the works of architecture which now mostly meet with misunderstanding or a certain aversion will become generally comprehensible, original, even popular.

Our living conditions, our constructions must be fully expressed if architecture is not to become a caricature of itself.

The realism of our epoch must penetrate the work of art. That won't do it any harm, won't result in the decline of art. Rather it will bring new pulsating life to the forms and, in time, will conquer new fields like engineering, which now still escape art. And only then can we speak of real development in art. I even maintain that thus we will be compelled to develop a representative style of our own.

Otto Wagner, 1894[2]

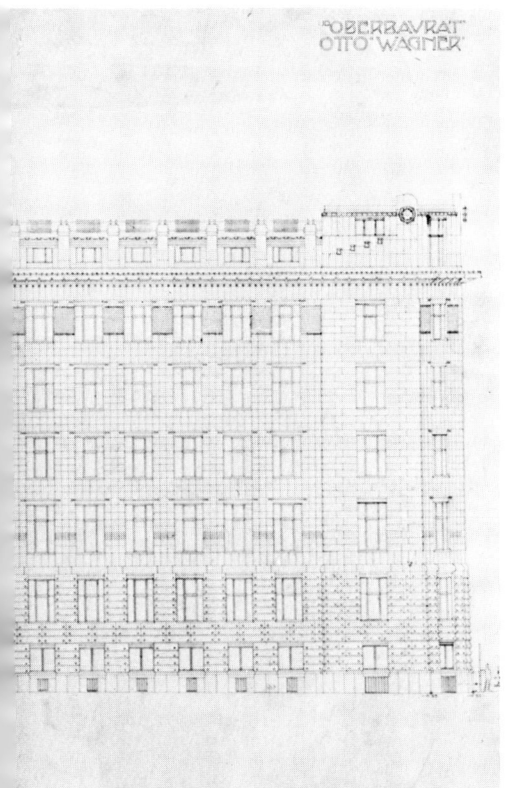

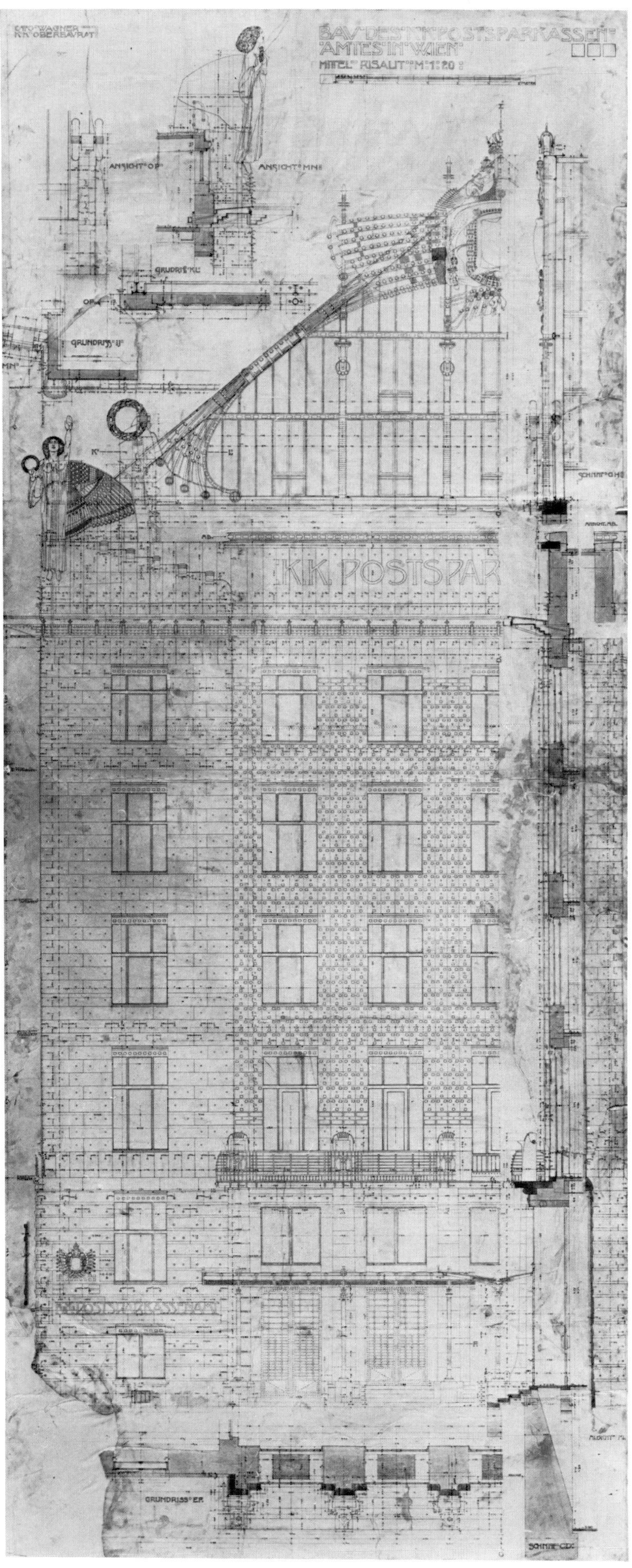

39
Otto Wagner
Postsparkassenamt. Werkzeichnung. Tusche und Aquarellfarbe
Postal Savings Bank. Working drawing. Drawing ink and water color

40
Otto Wagner
Ausschnitt aus Abbildung 39
Detail from illustration 39

FRANZ·JOSEF·I·DIE·STADT·WIEN·08
JUBILÄUMSBRUNNEN·AM·KARLSPLATZ
IN·DER·AXE·DER·WIENZEILE
OBERBAURAT
OTTO WAGNER
PERSPECTIVISCHE·ANSICHT

41
Otto Wagner
Jubiläumsbrunnen am Karlsplatz. Perspektivischer Aufriß. Bleistift, weiß gehöht
Jubilee Fountain at the Karlsplatz. Perspective elevation. Pencil, heightened with white

42
Otto Wagner
Karlsplatz mit Jubiläumsbrunnen. Perspektive. Bleistift und Deckweiß
Karlsplatz with Jubilee Fountain. Perspective. Pencil and zinc white

43
Otto Wagner
Kirche Am Steinhof. Perspektivskizze. Bleistift, Aquarell- und Goldfarbe
Kirche Am Steinhof. Perspective sketch. Pencil, water color and gold paint

44
Otto Wagner
Kirche Am Steinhof. Perspektive. Tusche und Aquarellfarbe
Kirche Am Steinhof. Perspective. Drawing ink and water color

45 (Seite/page 52)
Otto Wagner
Kirche Am Steinhof. Aufriß der Hauptfassade. Tusche
Kirche Am Steinhof. Elevation of the main façade. Drawing ink

46 (Seite/page 53)
Otto Wagner
Kirche Am Steinhof. Perspektivischer Aufriß des Hochaltars. Tusche und Bleistift
Kirche Am Steinhof. Perspective elevation of the high altar. Drawing ink and pencil

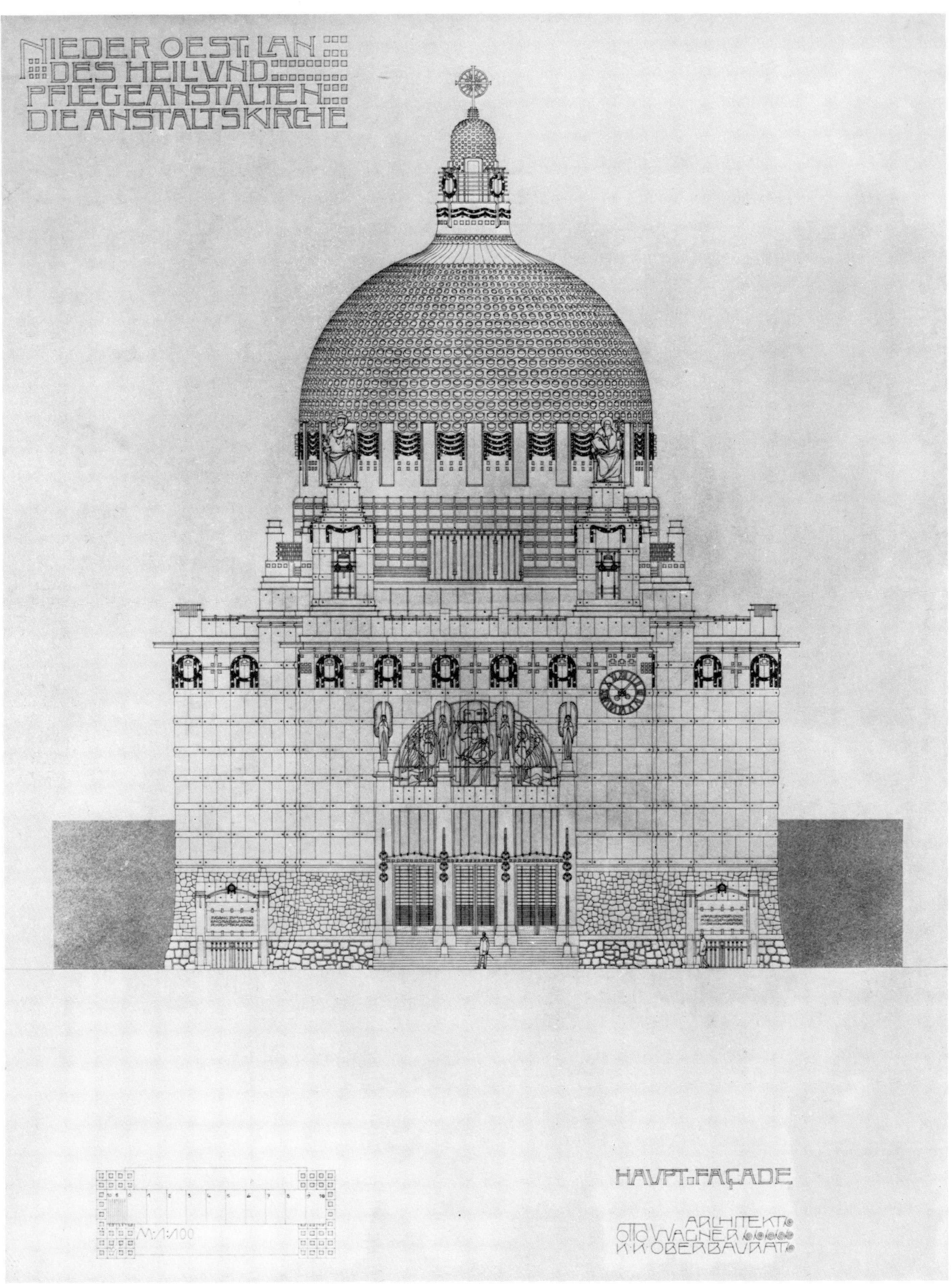
NIEDER OEST. LAN
DES HEIL. UND
PFLEGEANSTALTEN
DIE ANSTALTSKIRCHE
M:1:100
HAUPT FAÇADE
ARCHITEKT
OTTO WAGNER
K.K. OBERBAURAT

NIEDER OESTERREICHISCHE
LANDES HEIL- UND PFLEGE
ANSTALTEN
DIE ANSTALTSKIRCHE

OBERBAURAT OTTO WAGNER

DER HOCHALTAR

47 (Seite/page 54)
Otto Wagner
Interimskirche. Perspektivskizze. Bleistift und Farbstift
Temporary church. Perspective sketch. Pencil and crayon

48 (Seite/page 55)
Otto Wagner
Interimskirche. Perspektivskizze. Bleistift und Farbstift
Temporary church. Perspective sketch. Pencil and crayon

49
Otto Wagner
Interimskirche. Perspektivskizze des Innenraums. Bleistift und Farbstift
Temporary church. Perspective sketch of the interior. Pencil and crayon

50
Otto Wagner
Interimskirche. Perspektivskizze des Innenraums. Bleistift und Farbstift
Temporary church. Perspective sketch of the interior. Pencil and crayon

VILLA WAGNER

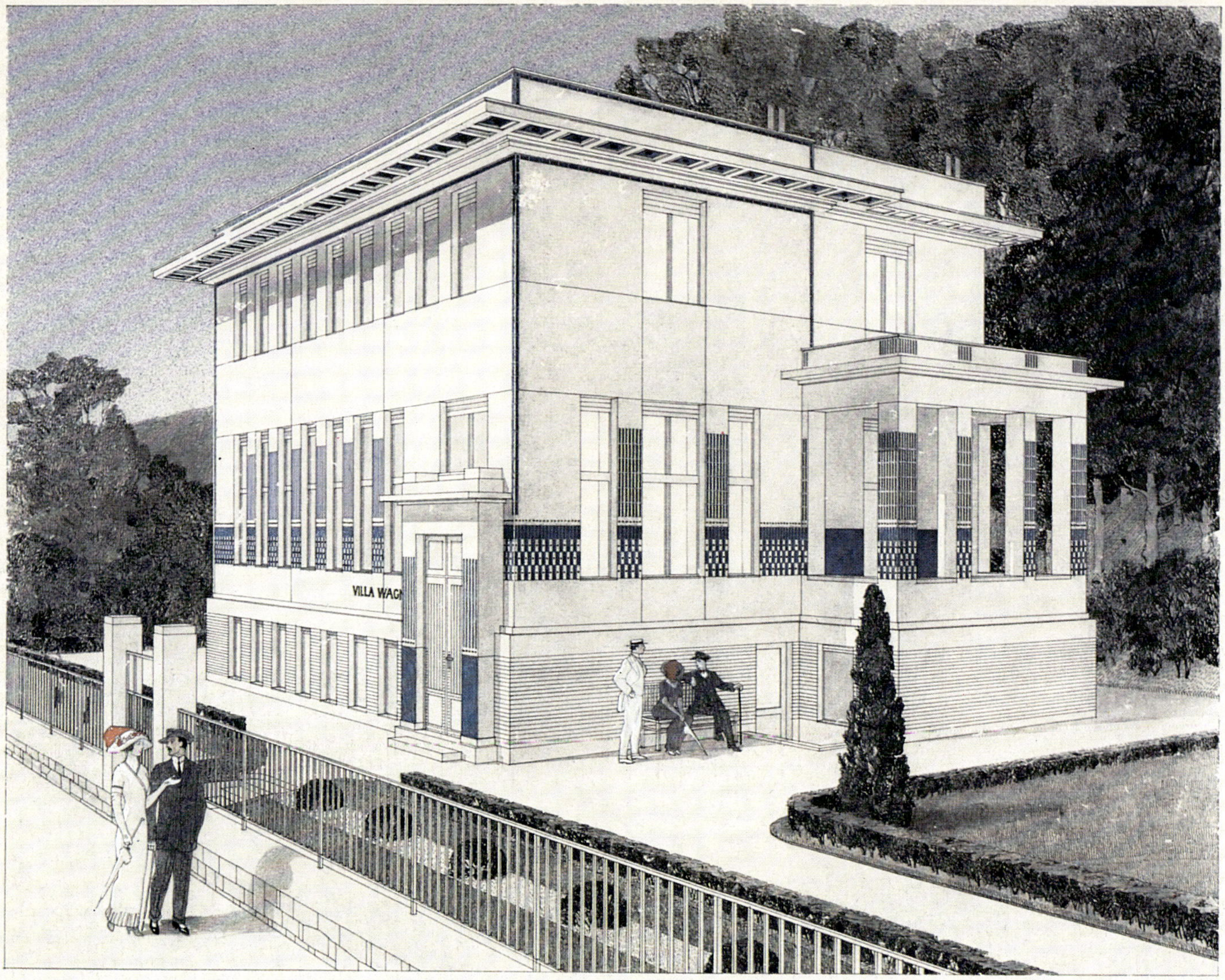

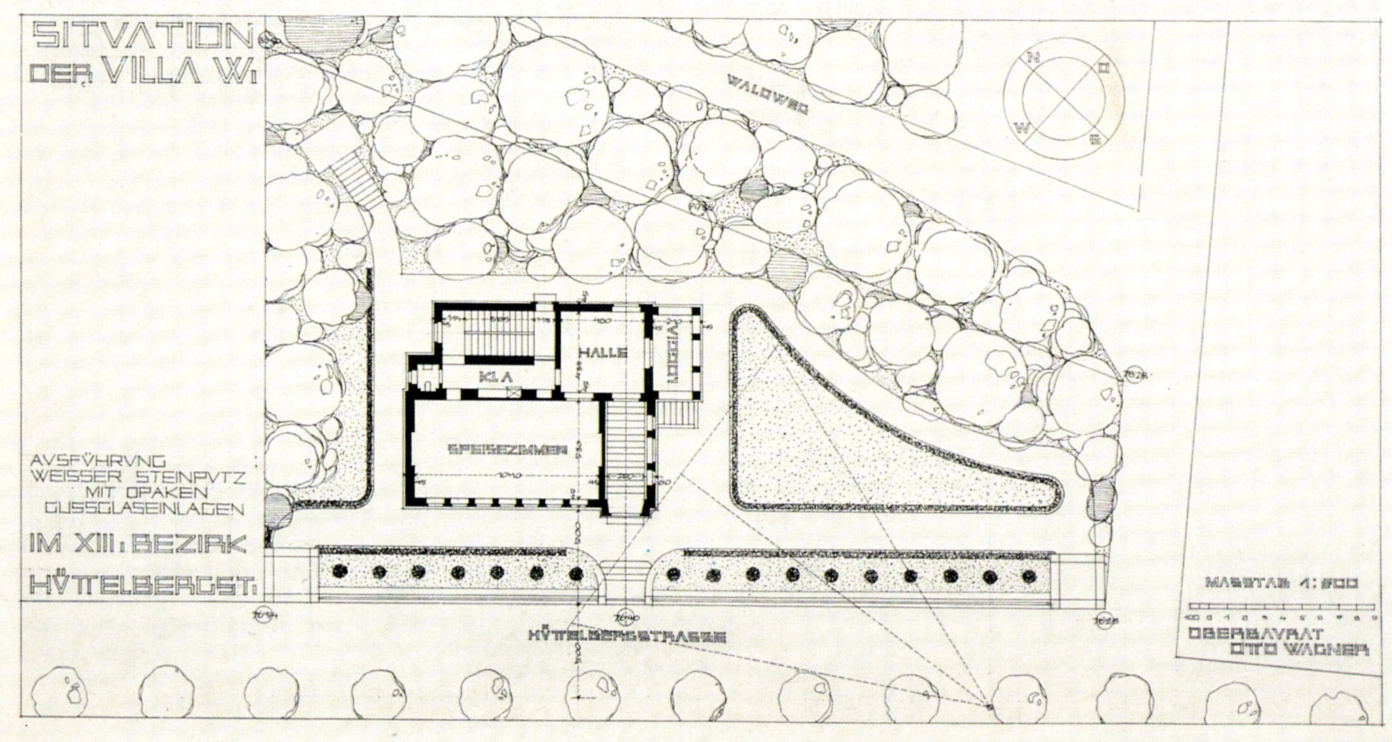

SITVATION
DER VILLA W.
WALDWEG
HALLE
LOGGIA
KLA
SPEISEZIMMER
AVSFÜHRVNG
WEISSER STEINPVTZ
MIT OPAKEN
GUSSGLASEINLAGEN
IM XIII. BEZIRK
HÜTTELBERGST.
HÜTTELBERGSTRASSE
MASSTAB 1:200
OBERBAVRAT
OTTO WAGNER

51
Otto Wagner
Villa Wagner. Perspektive und Grundriß. Tusche und Aquarellfarbe
Villa Wagner. Perspective and ground plan. Drawing ink and water color

52
Otto Wagner
Miethaus Neustiftgasse 40. Perspektive. Tusche
Tenement house, Neustiftgasse 40. Perspective. Drawing ink

53
Otto Wagner
Kaiser-Franz-Joseph-Stadtmuseum am Karlsplatz (3. Projekt). Perspektivskizze. Bleistift und Tusche, weiß gehöht
Kaiser-Franz-Joseph-Stadtmuseum at the Karlsplatz (third project). Perspective sketch. Pencil and drawing ink, heightened with white

54
Otto Wagner
Hotel am Karlsplatz. Perspektive. Tusche, Bleistift und Aquarellfarbe
Hotel at the Karlsplatz. Perspective. Drawing ink, pencil and water color

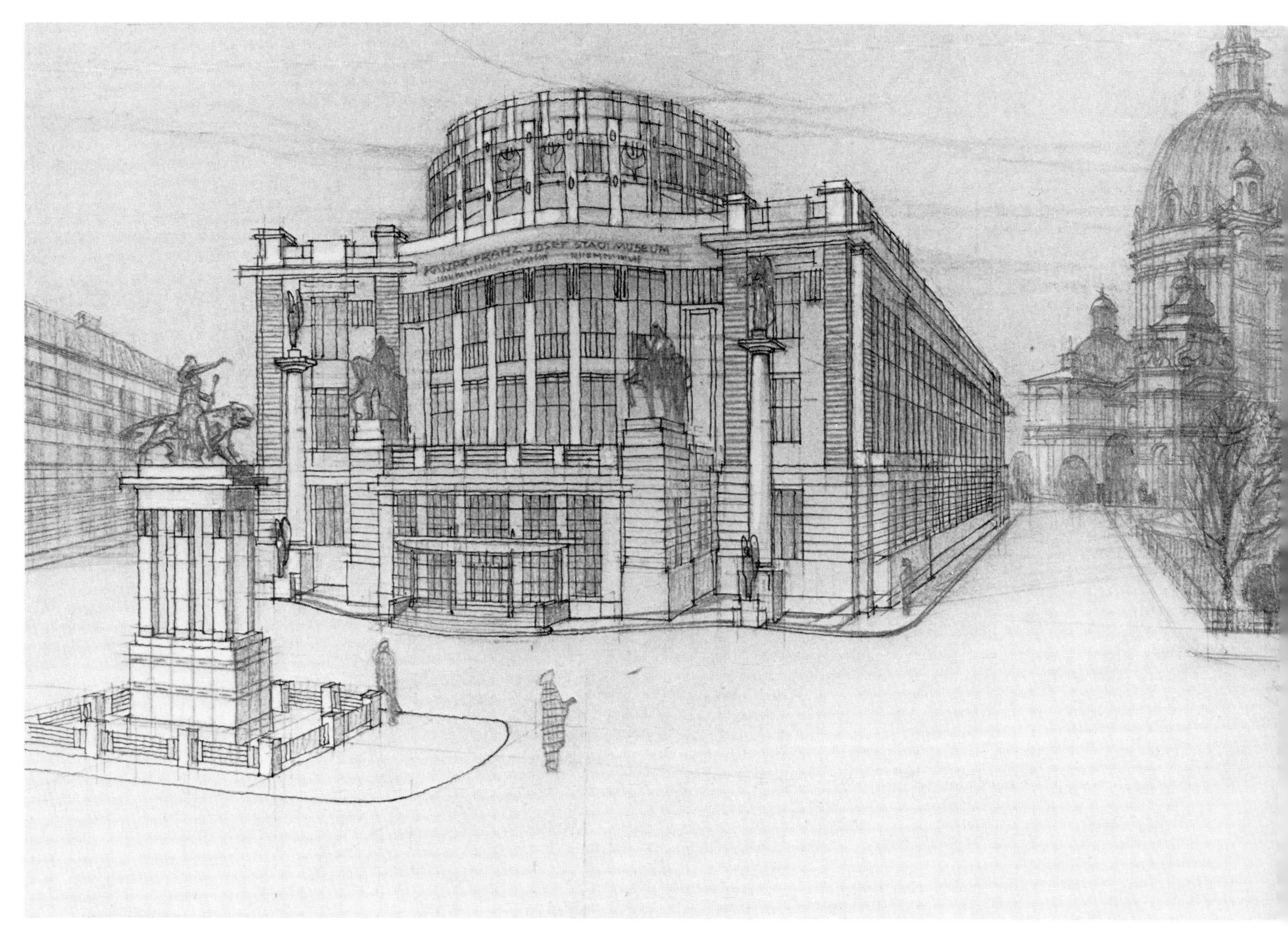

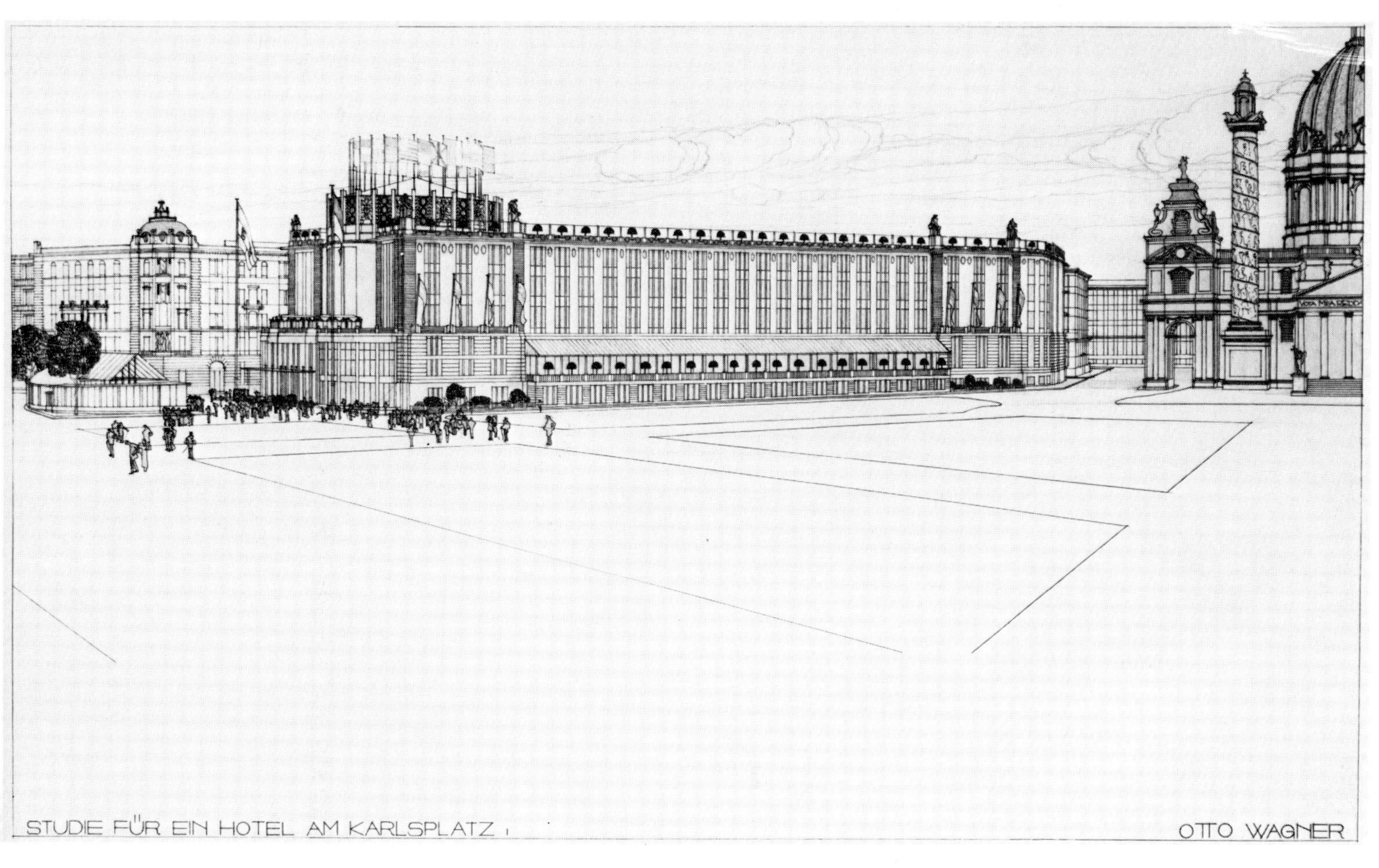

Here are the three principles on which the problem is based:
The house must function mechanically like a perfectly fashioned machine.
The furnishings should be of the quality of a wagon-lit.
As to hygiene and cleanliness, and utensils as well, it must meet clinical requirements.
In other words, a synthesis of clinic, wagon-lit, and machine. Perhaps we will achieve such first-rate hotels fifty years from now, if progress continues at today's rate. Consequently, it is clear that the problem is not good taste or artistic design, it is simply one of technical and constructive execution, of floor-plan solution, of demand for the greatest comfort reached with a minimal expenditure of time and means.
The technical servants and helpers in our life, the dumb-waiters, passenger and freight elevators, the light and bell installations, the cold- and hot-water pipes, the central heating, the telephone, all the mechanical and electrical systems which suffuse the house with nerve fibers, already give the whole installation a certain machine-like touch, quite apart from the downstairs kitchen, which looks like a boilerhouse, or the washing, utility and storage rooms in the basement.
. . . a house in this American style, anno 1950.

Joseph August Lux, 1909[3]

55
Otto Wagner
Idealentwurf des 22. Bezirks. Vogelperspektive. Tusche
Ideal design of the 22nd district. Bird's-eye view. Drawing ink

Wagner is above all an organizational talent with high aims. With a sure eye and extraordinary keenness he comprehends his task, one which he takes very seriously and into which he throws all his energy. He has a particular gift for ascertaining the requirements, recognizing the necessities, sacrificing nothing for form, a gift for organizing yet still taking account of the architectural image. That is why he is among the leading architects of the world.

Josef Hoffmann, 1910[4]

56
Otto Wagner
Kaiser-Franz-Joseph-Stadtmuseum auf der Schmelz. Perspektive. Tusche, weiß gehöht
Kaiser-Franz-Joseph-Stadtmuseum auf der Schmelz. Perspective. Drawing ink, heightened with white

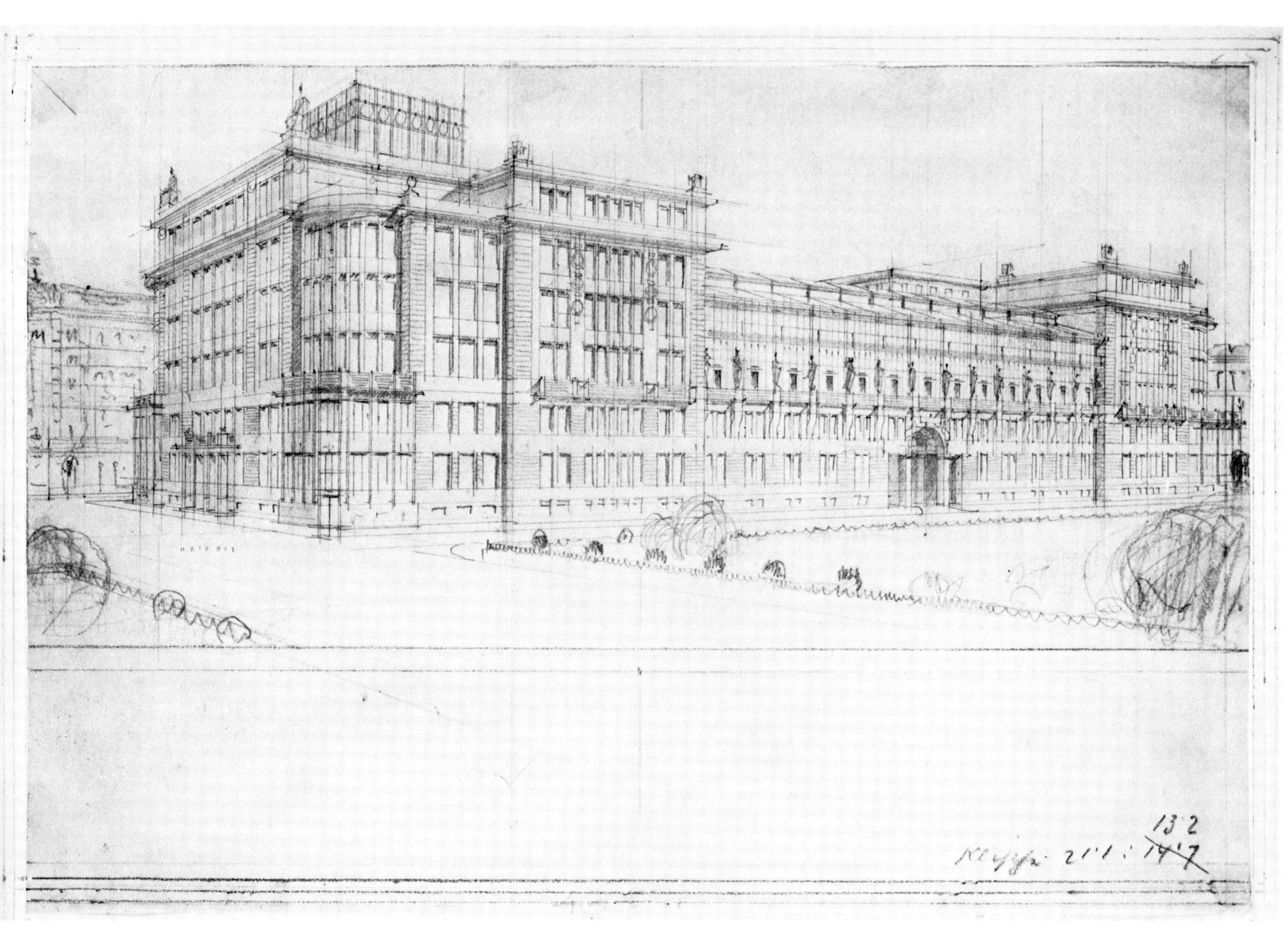

57
Otto Wagner
Ausstellungshallen. Perspektivskizze. Bleistift
Exhibition halls. Perspective sketch. Pencil

58
Otto Wagner
Sankt-Magdalenen-Spital. Aufriß eines Fassadenteils. Bleistift und Tusche, koloriert und weiß gehöht
Sankt-Magdalenen-Spital. Elevation of a part of the façade. Pencil and drawing ink, colored and heightened with white

59
Otto Wagner
Kaiser-Franz-Josephs-Stiftungs-Lazarett. Perspektive. Tusche
Kaiser-Franz-Josephs-Stiftungs-Lazarett. Perspective. Drawing ink

60
Joseph Maria Olbrich
Theaterprojekt. Perspektive. Tusche, Bleistift und Aquarellfarbe, weiß gehöht
Theater project. Perspective. Drawing ink, pencil and water color, heightened with white

Joseph M Olbrich
13. 7. 1893

61
Joseph Maria Olbrich
Franzensbrücke. Perspektivskizze mit gezeichnetem Passepartout. Tusche, laviert, und Aquarellfarbe
Franzensbrücke. Perspective sketch with drawn passepartout. Drawing ink with wash and water color

62
Joseph Maria Olbrich
Ausstellungsgebäude der Secession. Perspektivskizze des Haupteingangs. Bleistift, Tusche sowie Aquarell- und Deckfarbe
Secession exhibition building. Perspective sketch of the main entrance. Pencil, drawing ink, water color and poster paint

63
Joseph Maria Olbrich
Ausstellungsgebäude der Secession. Aufrißskizze der Hauptfassade. Tusche, laviert, und Aquarellfarbe, Gold gehöht
Secession exhibition building. Elevation sketch of the main façade. Drawing ink with wash and water color, heightened with gold

64
Joseph Maria Olbrich
Ausstellungsgebäude der Secession. Aufriß der Hauptfassade. Tusche und Aquarellfarbe
Secession exhibition building. Elevation of the main façade. Drawing ink and water color

AUSSTELLUNGS - GEBÄUDE
DER VEREINIGUNG BILDENDER KÜNSTLER OESTERREICHS

Gustav Klimt
Präsident

65
Joseph Maria Olbrich
Jubiläumspavillon der Stadt Wien. Aufriß- und Perspektivskizzen der Hauptfassade. Tusche und Bleistift
Jubilee Pavilion of the City of Vienna. Elevation and perspective sketches of the main façade. Drawing ink and pencil

66
Joseph Maria Olbrich
Stationsgebäude der Wiener Stadtbahn (?). Perspektivskizze. Tusche
Station building of the Viennese city railway (?). Perspective sketch. Drawing ink

67
Joseph Maria Olbrich
Pavillon des Radfahrclubs der Staats- und Hofbeamten. Aufriß, Grundriß und Schnitt. Tusche, Bleistift und Aquarellfarbe
Pavilion of the Radfahrclub der Staats- und Hofbeamten (Civil Servants' and Court Officials' Cycling Club). Elevation, ground plan and section. Drawing ink, pencil and water color

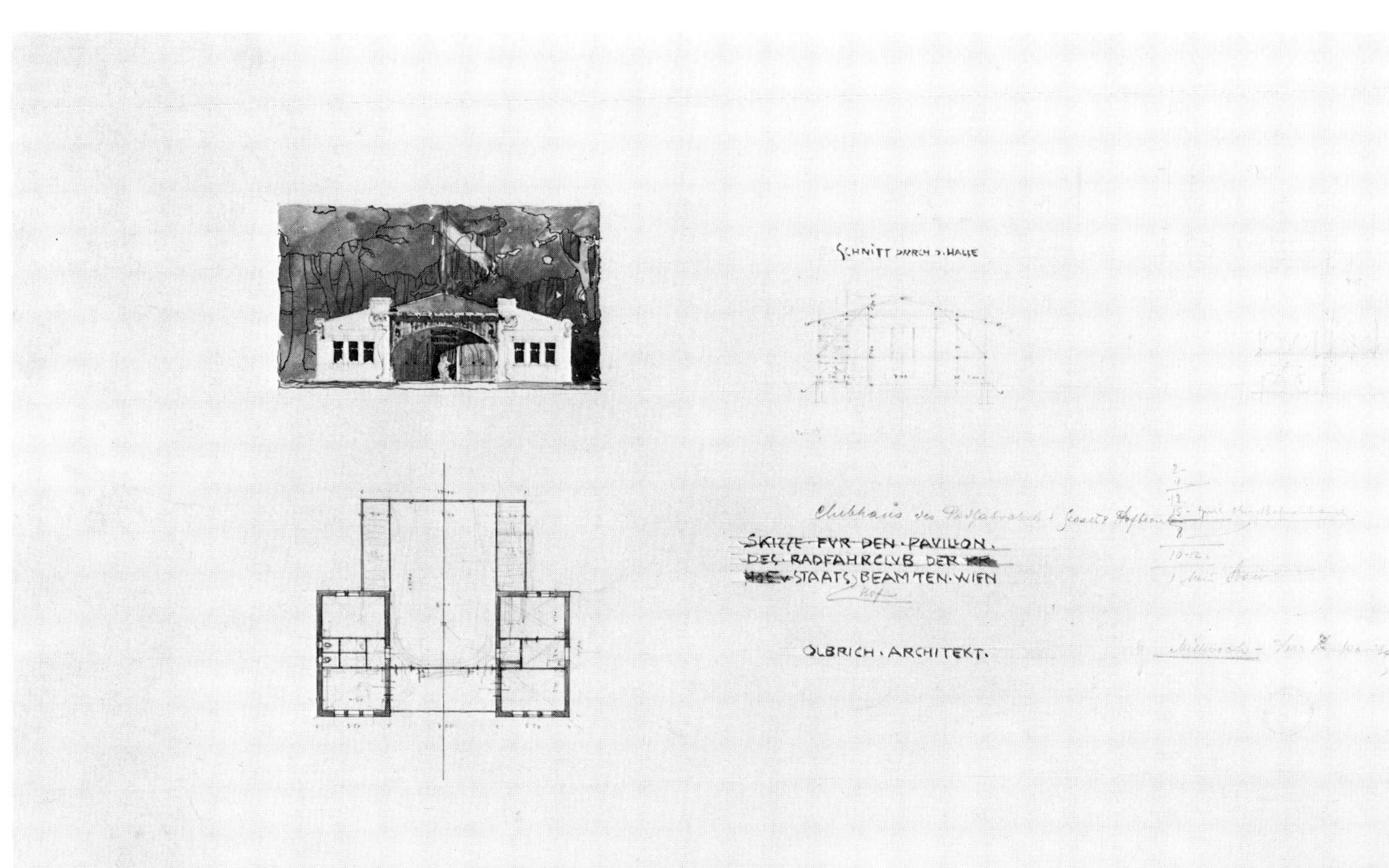

68
Joseph Maria Olbrich
Pavillon des Radfahrclubs der Staats- und Hofbeamten. Perspektivischer Aufriß der Hauptfassade. Tusche, Bleistift und Aquarellfarbe
Pavilion of the Radfahrclub der Staats- und Hofbeamten. Perspective elevation of the main façade. Drawing ink, pencil and water color

69
Joseph Maria Olbrich
Ausstellungsgebäude der Secession. Perspektive. Tusche und Aquarellfarbe
Secession exhibition building. Perspective. Drawing ink and water color

In 1893, my annual visit to the student exhibition of the Akademie, usually prompted by curiosity and a desire to ascertain the niveau of work, had an additional reason: I was looking for assistants to work on the architectural part of the city railway. Under Hasenauer's supervision, Olbrich had just completed a theater project for the exhibition (still absolutely traditional and typical Hasenauer), but thanks to its graphic perfection, it was even then superior to everything else. I made inquiries about this student and was informed that he was in the building. I met him in the vestibule and he immediately and with pleasure accepted my offer.

Since he had been granted the state traveling scholarship and had to prepare for his travels in the autumn, the three to four months' employment in my office were more than welcome to him. With one break, however (visit to Rome), these three to four months turned out to be five years.

This circumstance makes it possible for me to have exact knowledge of Olbrich's artistic career, to judge it correctly, and it induces me to pay tribute to him today. Among the many talents with which Olbrich was endowed (and which tended even then to more or less erupt), his vivid imagination, a strong poetical vein, a passionate, musical sensibility, accompanied by considerable musical ability, unusually good taste and an exceptional graphic dexterity must be particularly noted. As to construction and experience, he was a novice at the time. A mere few years were sufficient to perfect these skills and to raise all others to a level which I have never before observed in a man and am not likely to observe in the future.

As regards his manner, his style of representation, I can only compare him with one man, though hardly as an equal – my teacher van der Nüll.

All his qualities were supplemented by a considerable ambition which, backed up by his ability, made him look down mercilessly on his less gifted colleagues. This is a trait which I have only observed, though in more extreme form, in Gottfried Semper, whose intercourse with the world of art (unfortunately with good reason) culminated in his refusal to speak to anybody "because the crowd was too stupid" for him.

Otto Wagner, 1908[5]

70
Josef Plečnik
Wohnhaus. Perspektive. Bleistift und blaue Tinte
Residence. Perspective. Pencil and blue ink

71
Josef Plečnik
Palast. Perspektivskizze. Grüne Tinte und Farbstift
Palace. Perspective sketch. Green ink and crayon

72
Josef Plečnik
Fassadenstudie. Tusche
Façade study. Drawing ink

73
Josef Plečnik
Wohnhaus. Aufriß der Eingangsfassade und Grundriß. Tusche und Aquarellfarbe, ausgeschnitten und auf rotes Papier geklebt
Residence. Elevation of the entrance façade and ground plan. Drawing ink and water color, cut out and stuck onto red paper

74
Josef Hannich
Miethaus Wiednerhauptstraße. Aufriß. Bleistift und Tusche, koloriert
Tenement house, Wiednerhauptstrasse. Elevation. Pencil and drawing ink, colored

75
Josef Hannich
Miethaus Wiednerhauptstraße. Perspektive. Bleistift und Tusche, koloriert
Tenement house, Wiednerhauptstrasse. Perspective. Pencil and drawing ink, colored

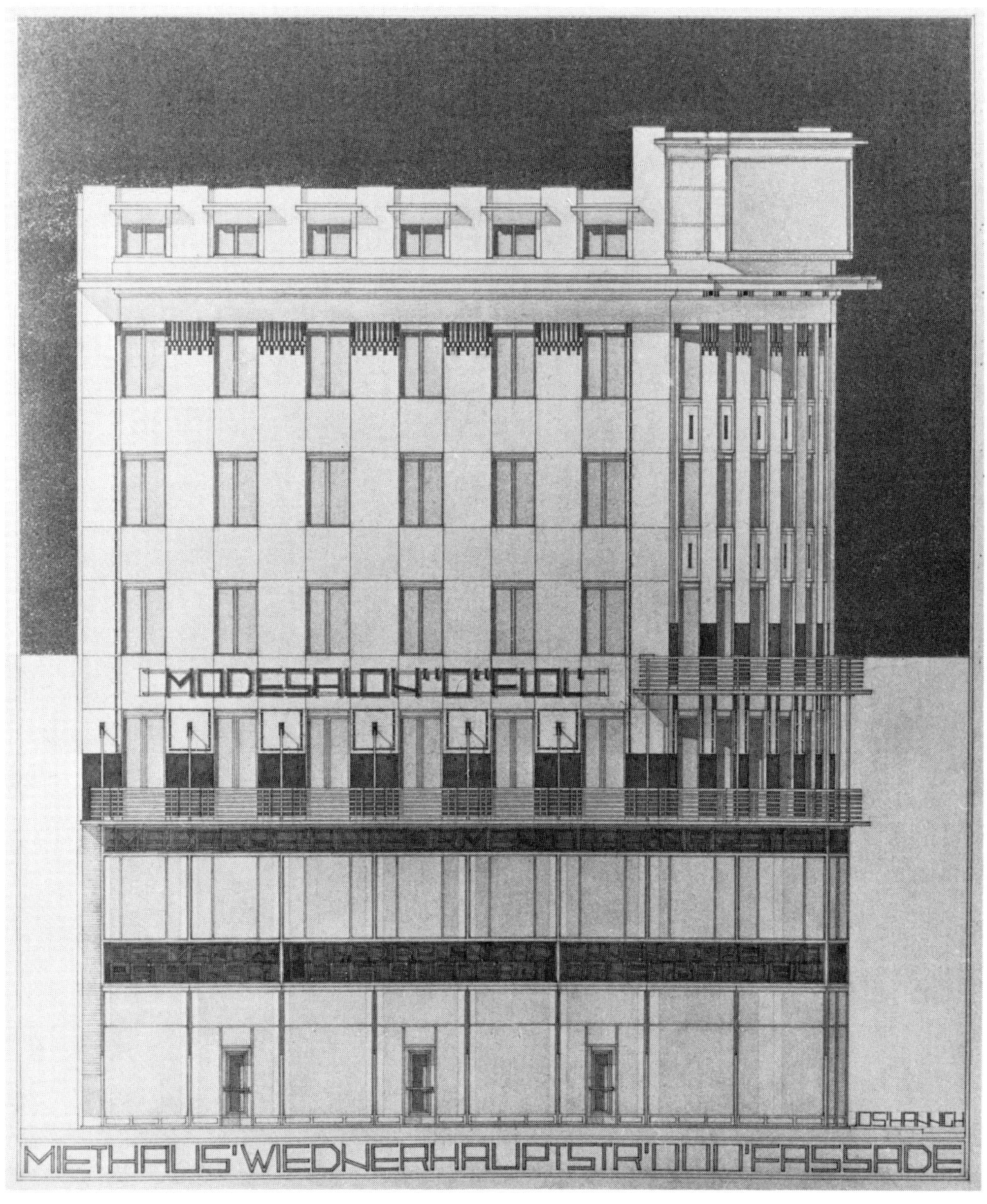

MODESALON
ROMANO
MODERNE
MIETHAUS'D'M
WIEDNERHSTR
IOS'HANNICH 1910

76
Josef Hannich
Häusergruppe in Weidling. Vogelperspektive. Tusche und Bleistift
Group of houses in Weidling. Bird's-eye view. Drawing ink and pencil

77
Josef Hannich
Haus Auhofstraße. Vogelperspektive. Tusche, Bleistift und Farbstift
House in the Auhofstrasse. Bird's-eye view. Drawing ink, pencil and crayon

78
Josef Hannich
Ausbau der Wiener Hofburg. Perspektive. Bleistift, Tusche und Deckweiß
Extension of the Vienna Hofburg. Perspective. Pencil, drawing ink and zinc white

79
Franz Kaym
Kloster. Perspektive und Grundriß. Bleistift, Tusche und Aquarellfarbe
Monastery. Perspective and ground plan. Pencil, drawing ink and water color

80
Franz Kaym
Landkirche. Perspektive und Grundriß. Bleistift, Farbstift, Tusche und Goldfarbe, weiß gehöht
Country church. Perspective and ground plan. Pencil, crayon, drawing ink and gold paint, heightened with white

81
Otto Schönthal
Wohnhaus. Perspektive. Bleistift und Aquarellfarbe
Residence. Perspective. Pencil and water color

82
Emil Hoppe/Marcel Kammerer/Otto Schönthal
Theaterraum. Perspektive. Bleistift und Aquarellfarbe
Theater hall. Perspective. Pencil and water color

83
Adolf Loos
Kaminnische. Perspektivskizze. Bleistift
Fireplace niche. Perspective sketch. Pencil

84
Adolf Loos
Interieur. Perspektivskizze. Tusche und Farbstift
Interior. Perspective sketch. Drawing ink and crayon

85
Adolf Loos
Gebäude im Stadtparkbereich. Perspektivskizze. Bleistift
Building in the Stadtpark area. Perspective sketch. Pencil

I meet the famous modern interior designer X in the street.
Good afternoon, I say, I saw one of your flats yesterday.
Oh yes – which one?
The one belonging to Dr. Y.
What! The one belonging to Dr. Y? For goodness sake, don't look at that rubbish, I did that three years ago.
You don't say! I have always thought there was a basic difference between us, dear colleague. Now I see that it is only a time difference. A time difference that can be expressed in years. Three years! That is, I maintained even then that it was rubbish – and it has taken you until today.

Adolf Loos, 1903[6]

The Papuan tattoos his skin, his boat, his oars, in short, everything within his reach. He is no criminal. The modern man who tattoos himself is a criminal or a degenerate. There are prisons in which eighty percent of the prisoners are tattooed. The tattooed men who are not in prison are latent criminals or degenerate aristocrats. If a tattooed man dies in freedom, then he has died just a few years before committing a murder.
Man's urge to ornament his face and everything within his reach is the prime origin of the fine arts. It is the babblings of painting. All art is erotic.
The cross, the first ornament to be born, was of erotic origin. The first work of art, the first artistic act which the first artist scribbled on the wall in order to get rid of his surplus energy. A horizontal line: the recumbent woman. A vertical line: the man penetrating her. The man who created it experienced the same urge as Beethoven, he was in the same heaven in which Beethoven created the Ninth.
But the man of our time who, due to some inner compulsion, smears the walls with erotic symbols, is a criminal or a degenerate. It goes without saying that this compulsion seizes men with such degenerate symptoms most frequently in public conveniences. The culture of a country can be measured by the amount of smearing on toilet walls. With a child it is a natural phenomenon: his first artistic manifestation is the scribbling of erotic symbols on walls. However, that which is natural with the Papuan and with the child is a sign of degeneration with the modern man. I have come to realize the following, which I have bestowed upon the world: *evolution of culture is equivalent to removing the ornament from the product.* With this I thought to have brought new joy to the world. I received no thanks for it. Everybody was sad and let his head hang. What depressed men was the realization that no new ornament could be created. ...
Since the ornament is no longer organically connected with our culture, it is therefore no longer the expression of our culture. The ornament created today has no connection with us, has no human connections at all, no connection with the world order. It is incapable of development. What happened to the ornamentation of Otto Eckmann, to that of Van de Velde? The artist, full of vigor and fitness, always stood at the peak of mankind. The modern ornamenter, however, is a straggler or a pathological phenomenon. He himself rejects his own products after a scant three years. People of culture find them intolerable right away, the others only become aware of the intolerability years later. Where are the works of Otto Eckmann today? Where will the works of Olbrich be ten years from now? Modern ornamentation has no parents and no descendants, has no past and no future. ...
The changing of ornaments results in a premature devaluation of the product. The worker's time, the material used, are wasted capital. I have laid down the dogma: an object should retain its form so long, that is, should be tolerable so long as it retains its physical condition. I shall attempt to explain this: a suit will alter its form more frequently than a valuable fur. The woman's ballgown, intended for one night only, will alter its form more quickly than a writing desk. But watch out when the desk has to be changed as frequently as a ballgown because the old form has become intolerable, for the money spent on the desk is then lost.
The ornamenter knows this well, and the Austrian ornamenters are attempting to take advantage of this situation. They say: "A consumer who finds his furnishings intolerable after ten years, and is thus forced to refurnish every ten years, is preferable to us than one who only buys a new article when the old one is worn out. Industry demands this. Millions of people find employment as a result of this rapid change." This appears to be the secret of the Austrian political economy; when a fire breaks out, how often do we hear the words: "Thank goodness, now people have something to do again." I have a good recipe for this: set fire to a town, set fire to the empire and everything will swim in money and prosperity.

Manufacture furniture which can be used as firewood three years later, fittings which must be melted down after four years because even at auction they would not fetch a tenth of the labor and material costs, and we'll become richer and richer. ...
I preach to the aristocrats. I endure ornaments on my own body if they give pleasure to my fellows. They are then my pleasure too. I endure the ornaments of the Kafir, of the Persian, of the Slovak peasant woman, the ornaments of my cobbler, for they all have no other means of reaching the climax of their existence. We have the arts which have replaced the ornament. After the daily trials and burdens we go to Beethoven or Tristan. My cobbler cannot do this. I dare not rob him of his pleasure, for I have nothing to replace it with. But whoever goes to the Ninth Symphony and then sits down to draw a wallpaper pattern is either a fraud or a degenerate.
The absence of the ornament has brought the other arts to an undreamed of height. Beethoven's symphonies would never have been written by a man who had to walk about in silk, velvet and lace. Whoever runs around in a velvet jacket today is not an artist but a clown or a house painter.

Adolf Loos, 1908[7]

Architecture has been degraded to a graphic art by the architect. The most contracts are not given to the one who builds best, but to the one whose designs look best on paper. And those two are antipodes.
If we place the arts in a row and begin with the graphic arts, we find that there are gradations from them to painting. From it we can go to plastic art by way of colored sculpture, and from the plastic art to architecture. Graphic arts and architecture are the beginning and the end of a row.
The best draftsman can be a bad architect, the best architect a bad draftsman. A talent for graphics is required at the very choosing of architecture as a profession. Our entire new architecture has been contrived on the drawing-board, and the resulting drawings are given three-dimensional form, much in the way paintings are displayed in the panopticum.
To the old masters, however, the drawing was merely a means of making themselves understood to the craftsman who does the work – just as the poet must make himself understood through the written text. But we are not yet so devoid of culture that we would let a boy with calligraphic handwriting learn to write poetry.
For we all know: each work of art is subject to such rigid internal laws that it can only appear in one single form.

Adolf Loos, 1910[8]

Our culture is based on the acknowledgement of the sovereign greatness of classical antiquity. We have taken our way of thinking and feeling from the Romans. From the Romans we have our social perceptions and the discipline of the soul.
From the time that man became aware of the greatness of classical antiquity, one thought united the great architects. They thought: faced with the same task, the ancient Romans would have built in exactly the same manner as I have. I shall implant this thought into the minds of my students.
Today will build on yesterday, just as yesterday built on the day before.
It has never been otherwise – it will never be otherwise. This is the truth that I teach. As a result of the false doctrines which have taken hold of all schools and the general public, I shall never experience the victory of truth.

Adolf Loos, 1913[9]

86
Adolf Loos
Denkmal für Kaiser Franz Joseph. Aufrißskizze. Bleistift
Monument to Kaiser Franz Joseph. Elevation sketch. Pencil

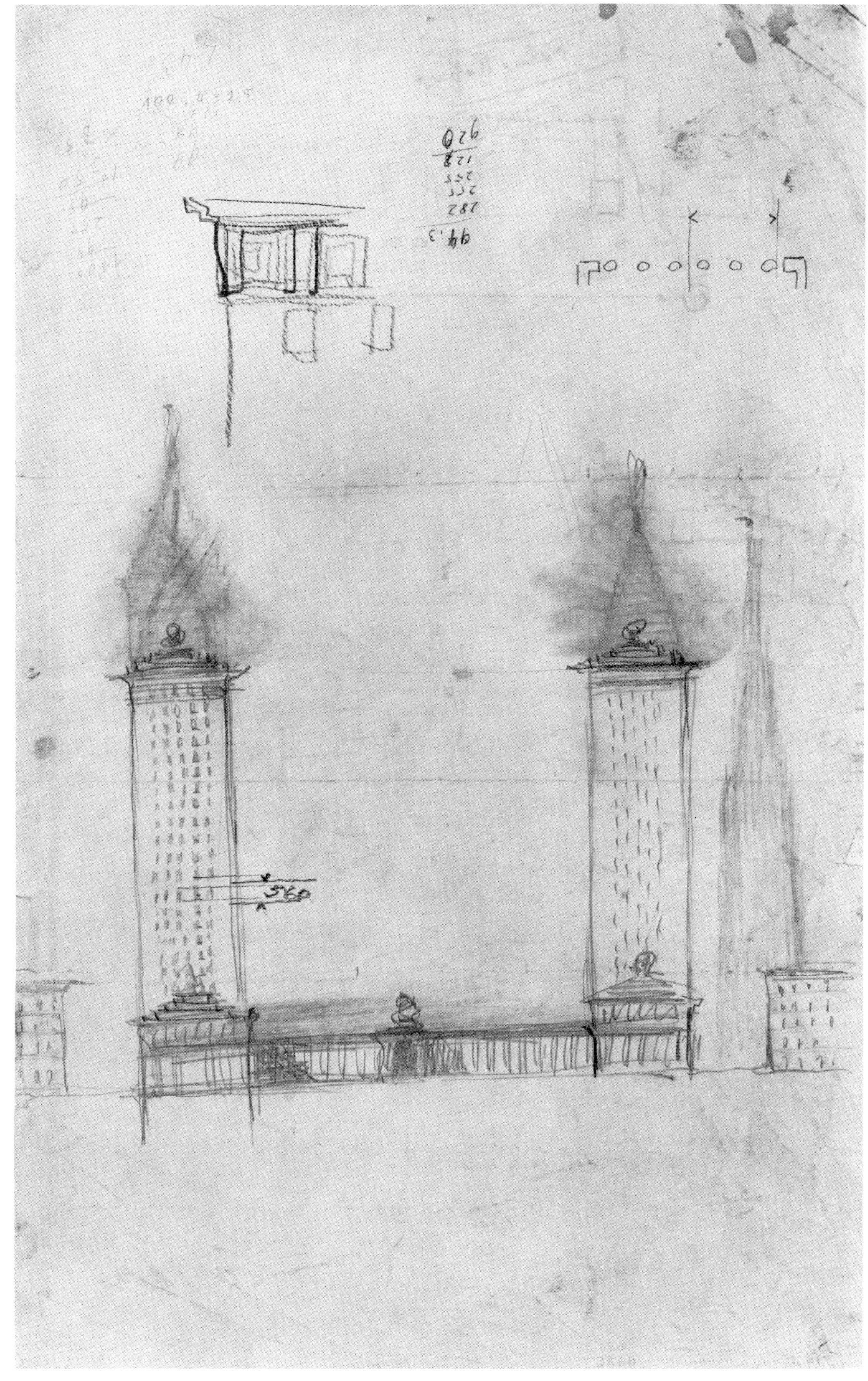

The value of artistic work and the idea will once again be recognized and appreciated. The work of the craftsman will be judged by the same standard as that of the painter and the sculptor. We neither can nor want to compete with cheapness; the worker is the one who will suffer, and we consider it our foremost duty to restore his enjoyment of work and to provide him with a decent existence. All this can only be achieved step by step.

Josef Hoffmann, 1904[10]

87
Josef Hoffmann
Bett. Perspektive. Tusche
Bed. Perspective. Drawing ink

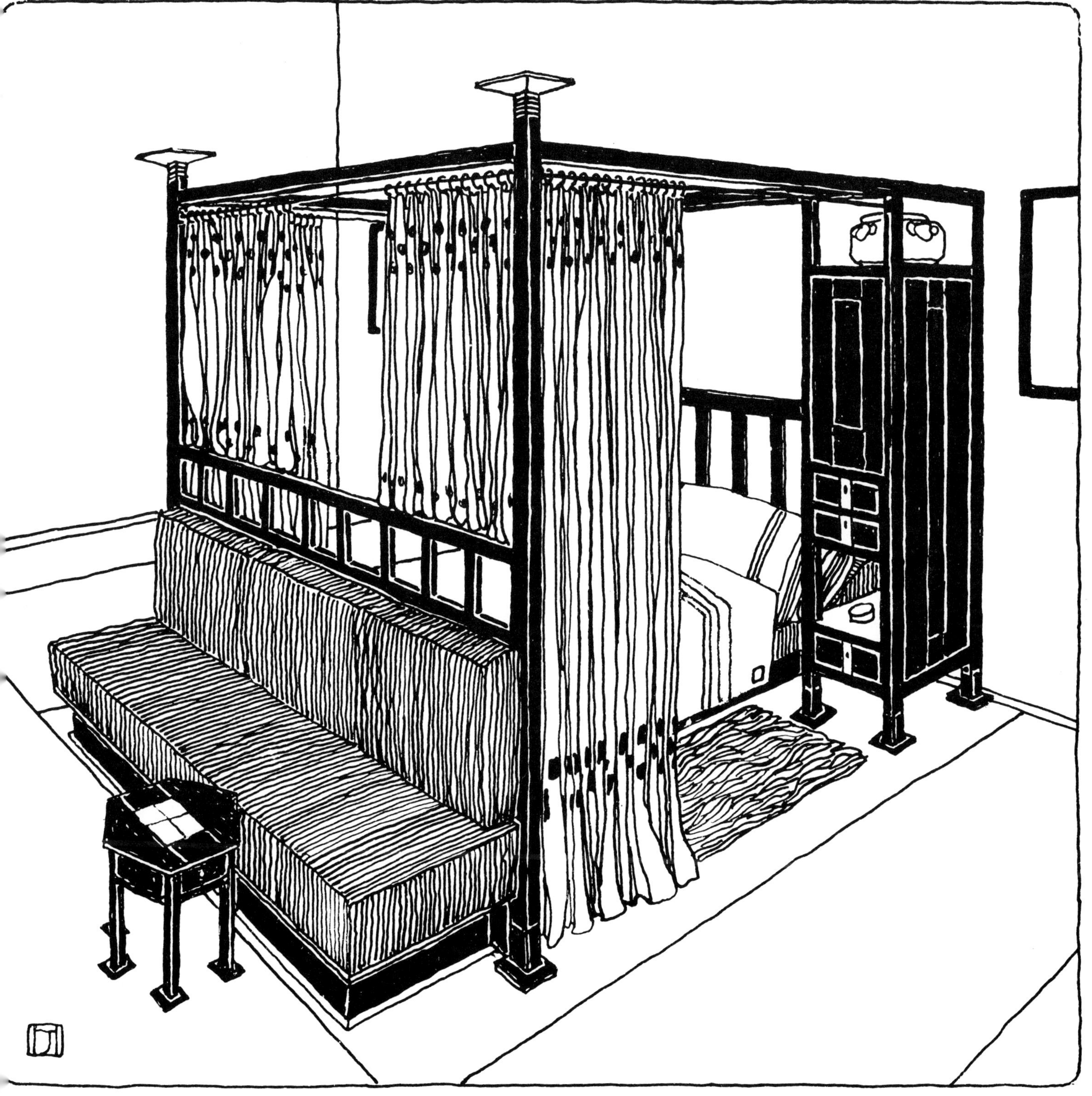

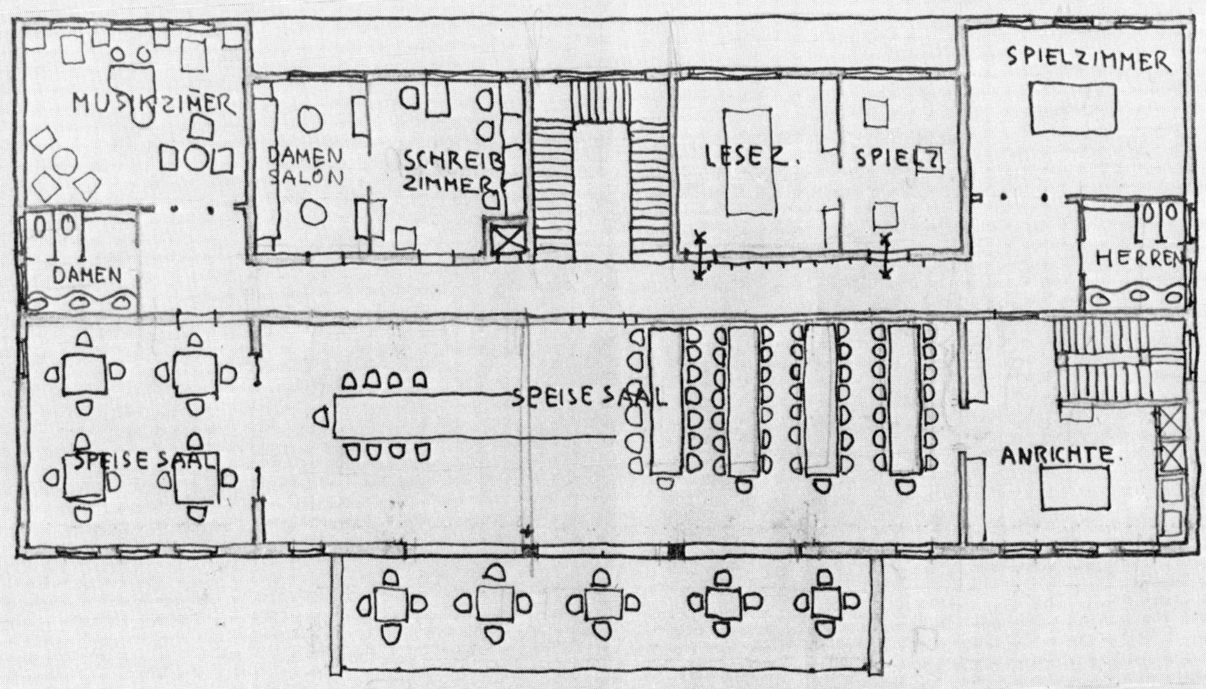

88
Josef Hoffmann
Sanatorium Purkersdorf. Grundrißskizze. Tusche, Bleistift und Farbstift
Purkersdorf Sanatorium. Ground plan sketch. Drawing ink, pencil and crayon

89
Josef Hoffmann
Sanatorium Purkersdorf. Aufrißskizze. Tusche und Bleistift
Purkersdorf Sanatorium. Elevation sketch. Drawing ink and pencil

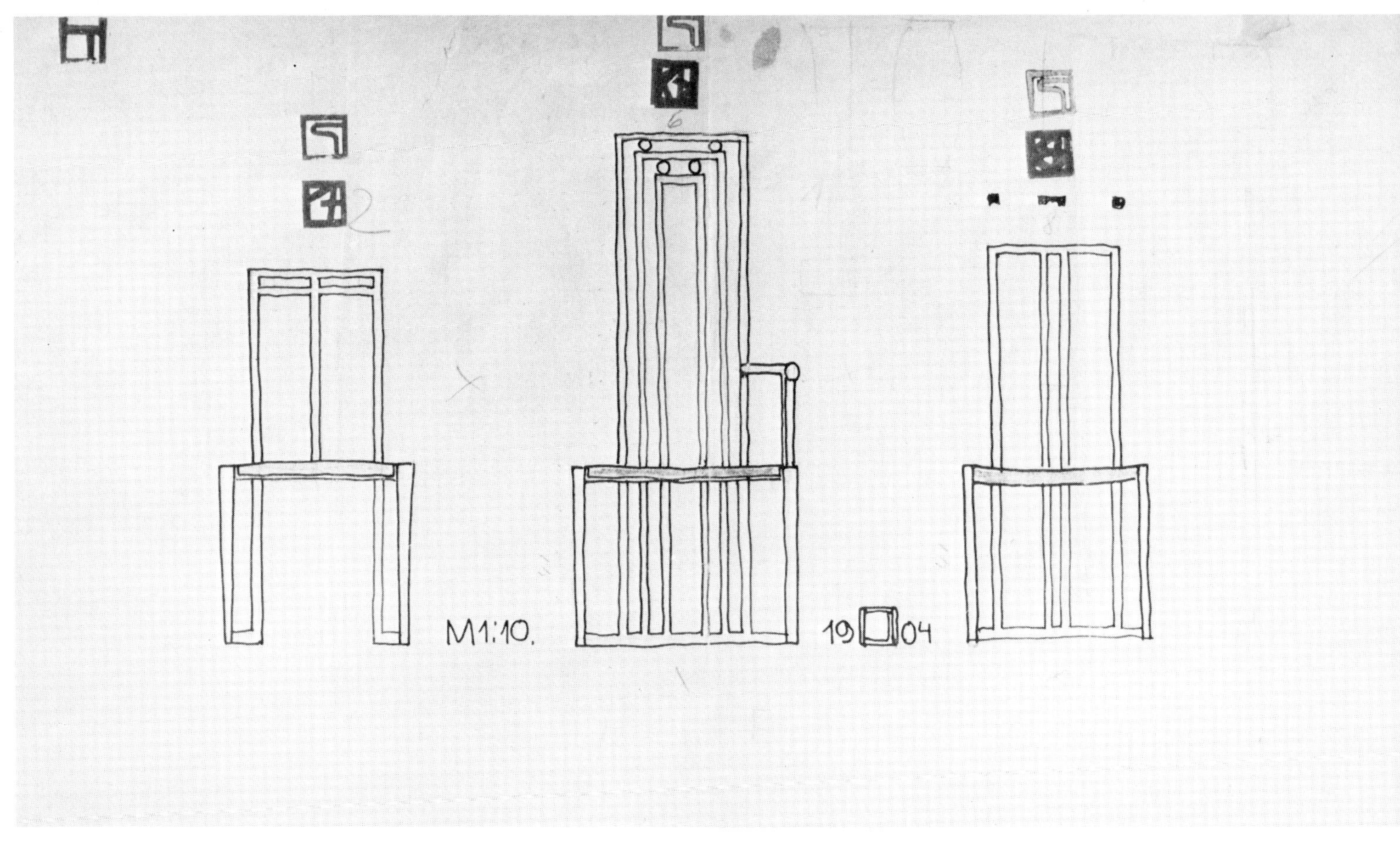

The unbounded evil which bad mass production, on the one hand, and thoughtless imitation of ancient styles, on the other, have inflicted upon the field of applied art is sweeping the entire world like a huge stream. We have lost contact with the culture of our forefathers and are tormented by thousands of wishes and considerations. The machine is taking the place of the hand, the businessman that of the artisan. It would be madness to swim against this stream. Nevertheless, we have set up our workshop. It shall be our resting point on native soil, amidst the cheerful noise of handicraft, and shall welcome those who embrace Ruskin and Morris. We appeal to all those who value a culture of this type, and hope that unavoidable mistakes will not deter our friends from supporting our intentions.

We wish to establish a close contact between the public, designer and artisan, and to produce good, simple household goods. Our first consideration is function, usability is our primary stipulation, good proportions and correct treatment of material will be our strong points. We will ornament where appropriate, but without compulsion and not just for its own sake.

Josef Hoffmann, 1904[11]

90
Josef Hoffmann
Stühle. Aufrißskizzen. Tusche, Bleistift und Farbstift
Chairs. Elevation sketches. Drawing ink, pencil and crayon

91
Josef Hoffmann
Tisch mit Spiegel und Hocker. Ideenskizze. Bleistift
Table with mirror and stool. Concept sketch. Pencil

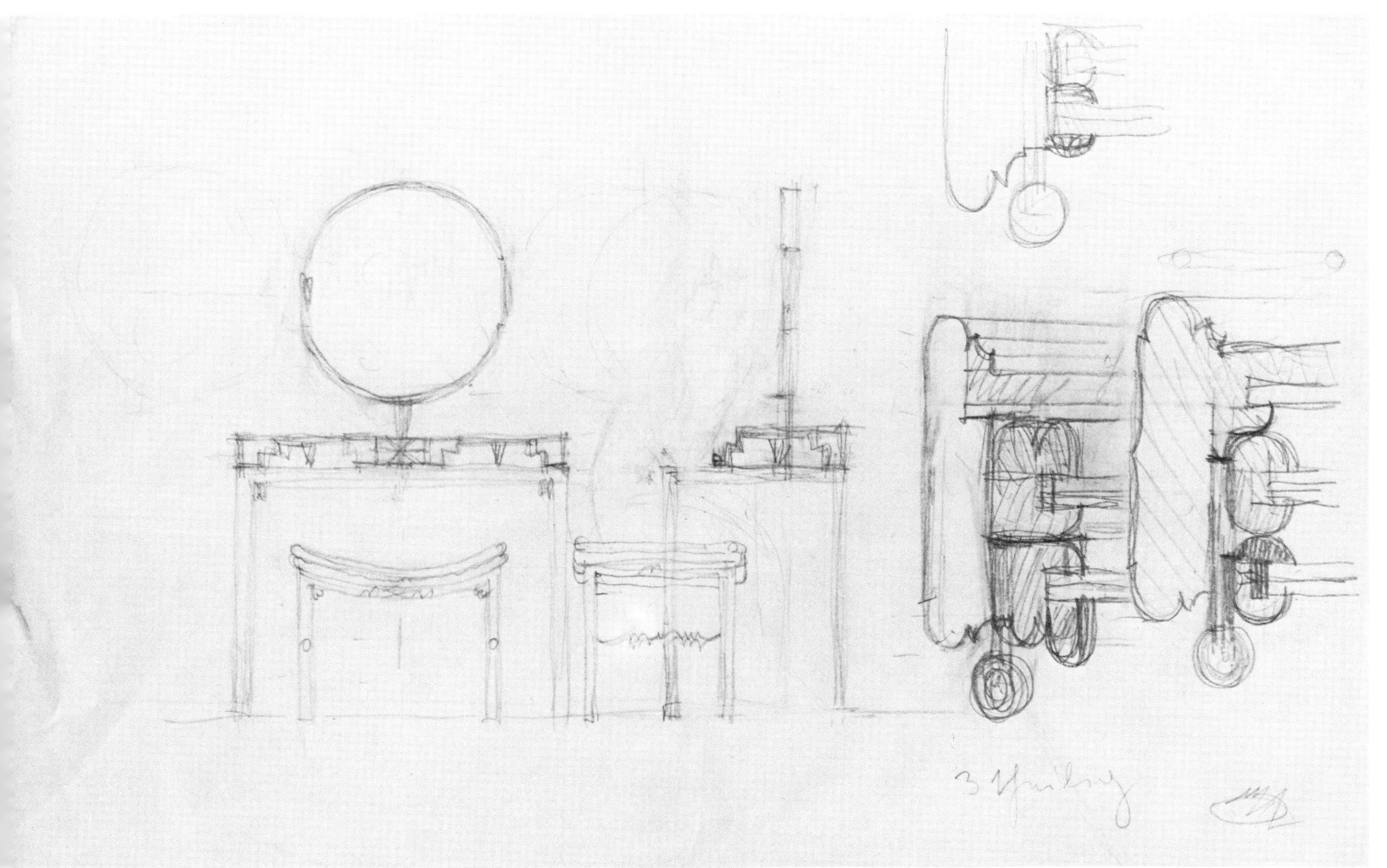

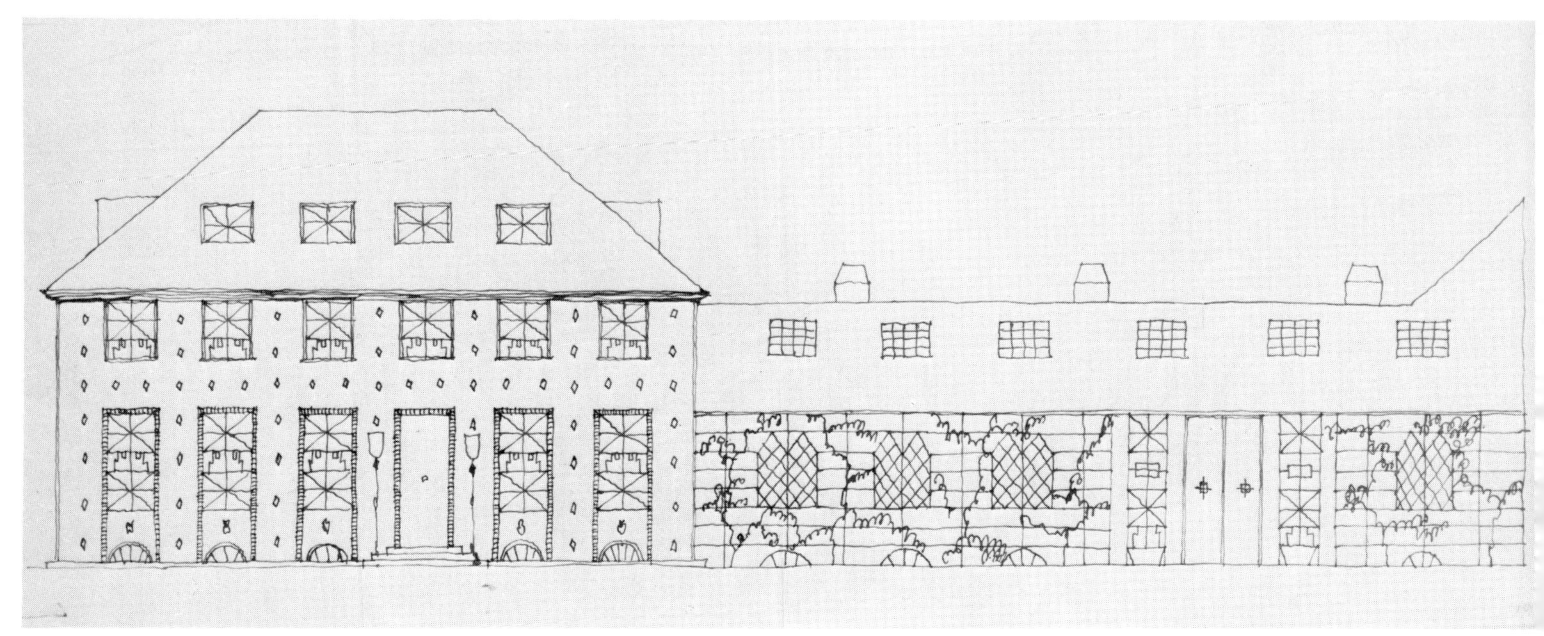

92
Josef Hoffmann
Haus Knips. Aufrißskizze der Eingangsfassade. Tusche
Knips House. Elevation sketch ot the entrance façade. Drawing ink

93
Josef Hoffmann
Klosehof. Aufrißskizze. Tusche
Klosehof. Elevation sketch. Drawing ink

94
Josef Hoffmann
Hochhaus. Aufrißskizze. Bleistift
High-rise building. Elevation sketch. Pencil

95
Josef Hoffmann
Wohnhaus. Aufrißskizze. Bleistift, Tusche und Aquarellfarbe
Residential house. Elevation sketch. Pencil, drawing ink and water color

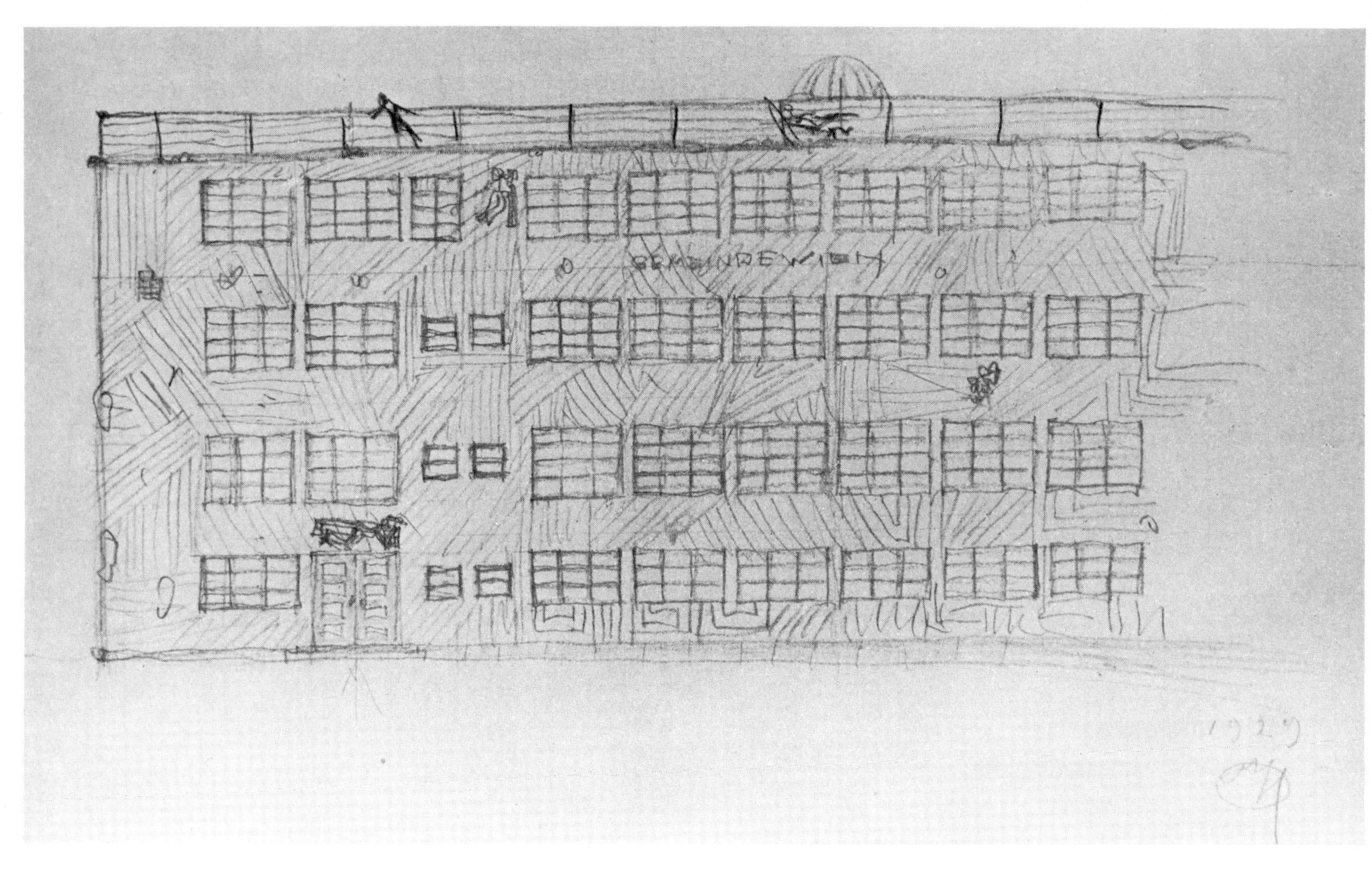

96
Josef Hoffmann
Wohnhaus für die Gemeinde Wien. Aufrißskizze.
Bleistift
Residential house for the Municipality of Vienna.
Elevation sketch. Pencil

97
Josef Hoffmann
Haus für die Werkbundsiedlung. Aufrißskizzen.
Bleistift und Farbstift
House for the Werkbund housing estate. Elevation sketches. Pencil and crayon

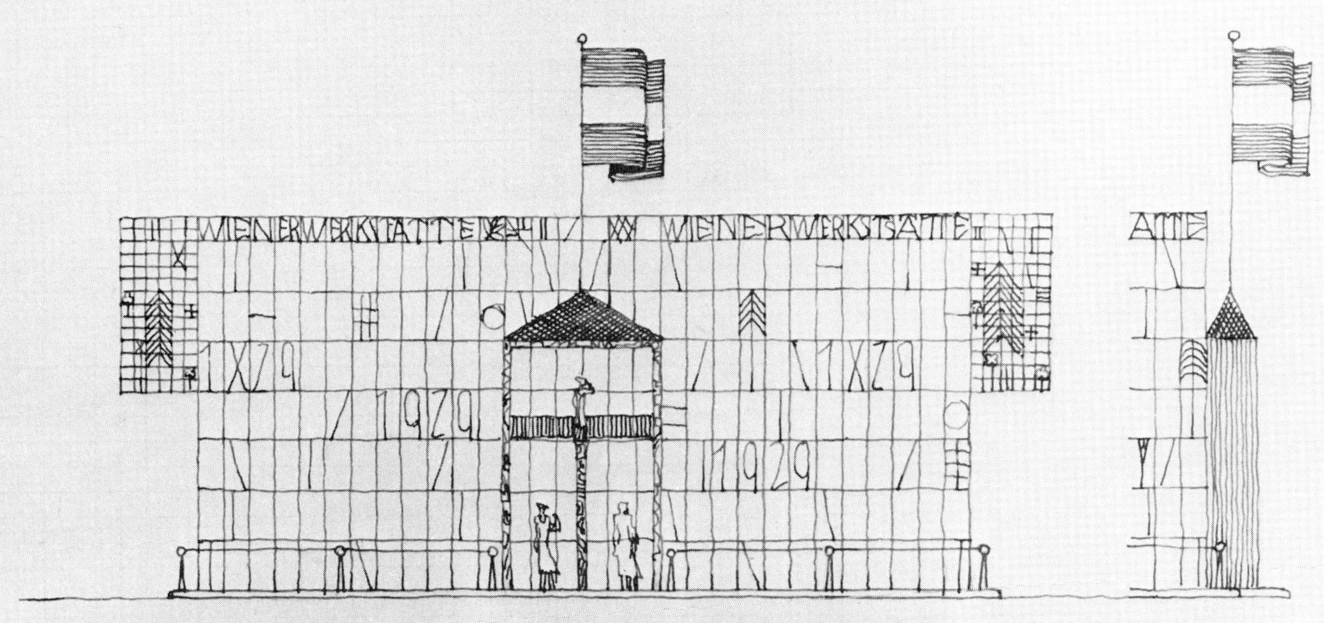

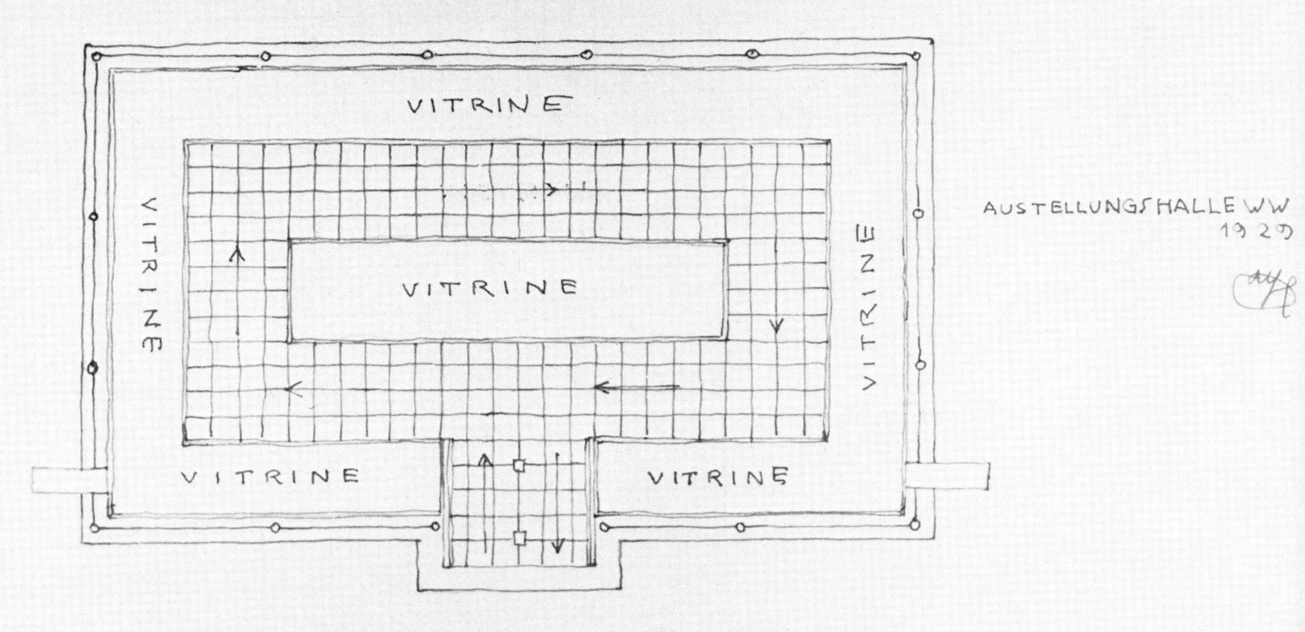

AUSTELLUNGSHALLE WW
1929

98
Josef Hoffmann
Ausstellungshalle der Wiener Werkstätte. Grundriß- und Aufrißskizze. Tinte
Exhibition hall of the Wiener Werkstätte. Sketch of ground floor and elevation. Ink

99
Josef Hoffmann
Gartenpavillon. Aufrißskizze. Tinte
Garden pavilion. Elevation sketch. Ink

STRNAD.

100
Oskar Strnad
Kriegsministerium (Wettbewerbsprojekt). Perspektive. Tusche und Aquarellfarbe
War Ministry (competition project). Perspective. Drawing ink and water color

101
Oskar Strnad
Wandabwicklungen. Tusche
Projections of walls. Drawing ink

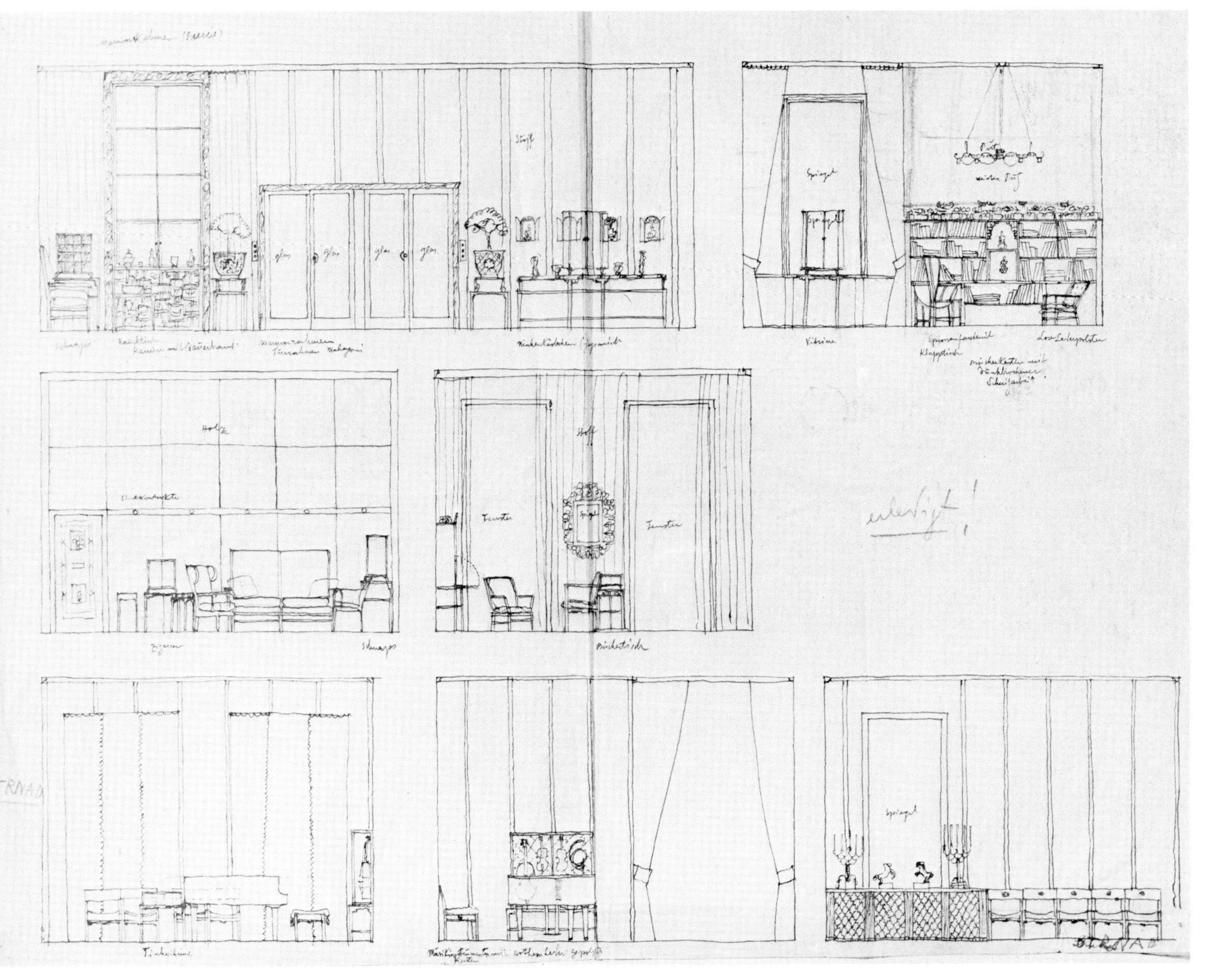

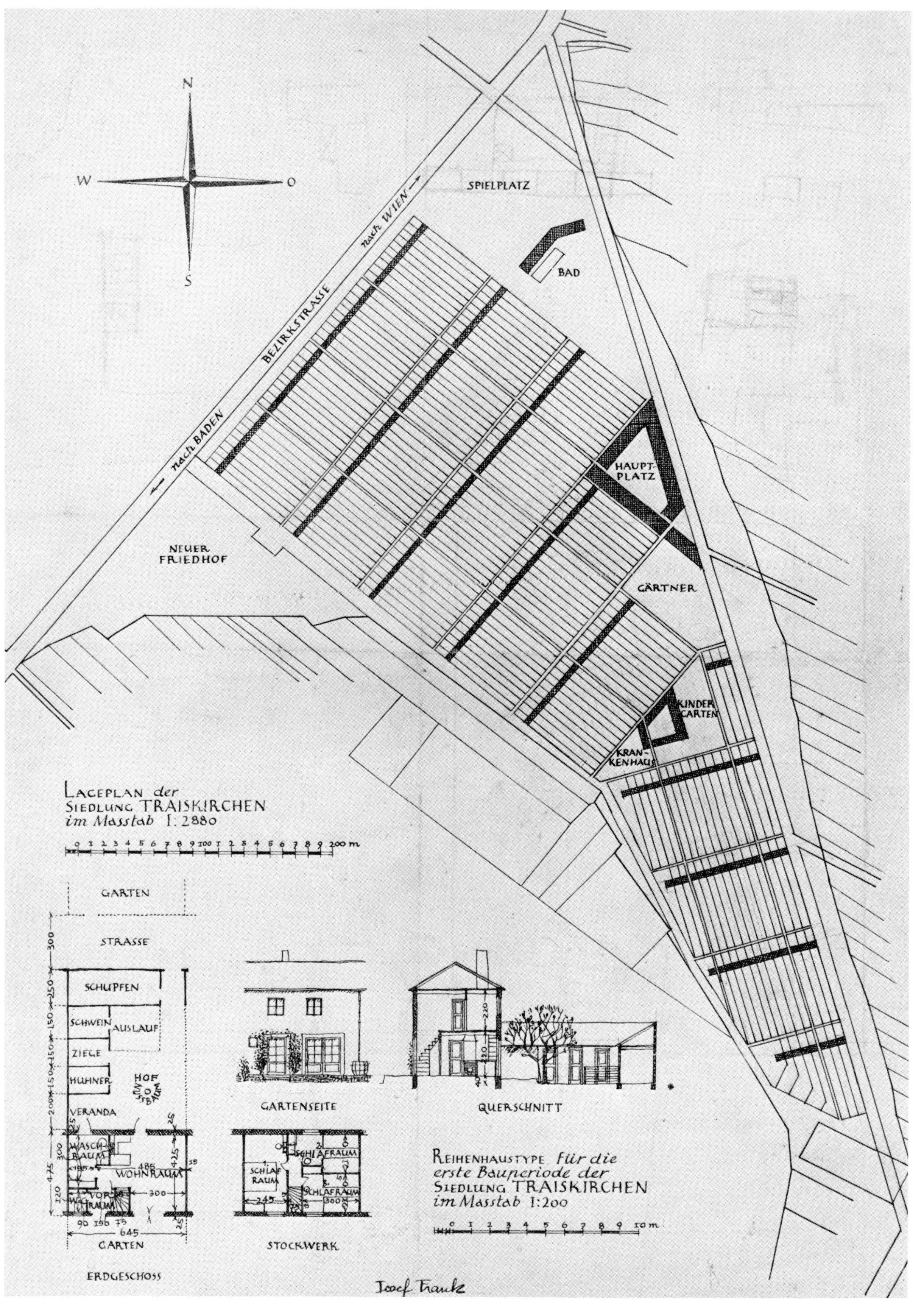
N
W
O
S
SPIELPLATZ
nach WIEN
BAD
BEZIRKSSTRASSE
nach BADEN
HAUPT-
PLATZ
NEUER
FRIEDHOF
GÄRTNER
KINDER
GARTEN
KRAN-
KENHAUS
LAGEPLAN der
SIEDLUNG TRAISKIRCHEN
im Masstab 1:2880
GARTEN
STRASSE
SCHUPFEN
SCHWEIN
AUSLAUF
ZIEGE
HÜHNER
HOF
VERANDA
WASCH
RAUM
WOHNRAUM
VOR
RAUM
GARTEN
ERDGESCHOSS
GARTENSEITE
SCHLAF
RAUM
SCHLAFRAUM
STOCKWERK
QUERSCHNITT
REIHENHAUSTYPE für die
erste Bauperiode der
SIEDLUNG TRAISKIRCHEN
im Masstab 1:200
Josef Frank

102
Josef Frank
Siedlung Traiskirchen. Lageplan der Siedlung und Pläne eines Reihenhauses (Grundrisse, Aufriß und Schnitt). Tusche
Traiskirchen housing estate. Site plan of the estate and plans of a terrace house (floor plans, elevation and section). Drawing ink

103
Josef Frank
Wohnhaus in Spittal/Drau. Lageskizze, Grundrisse, Schnitt, Aufriß und Perspektive. Tusche
Residence in Spittal/Drau. Sketch of site, floor plans, section, elevation and perspective. Drawing ink

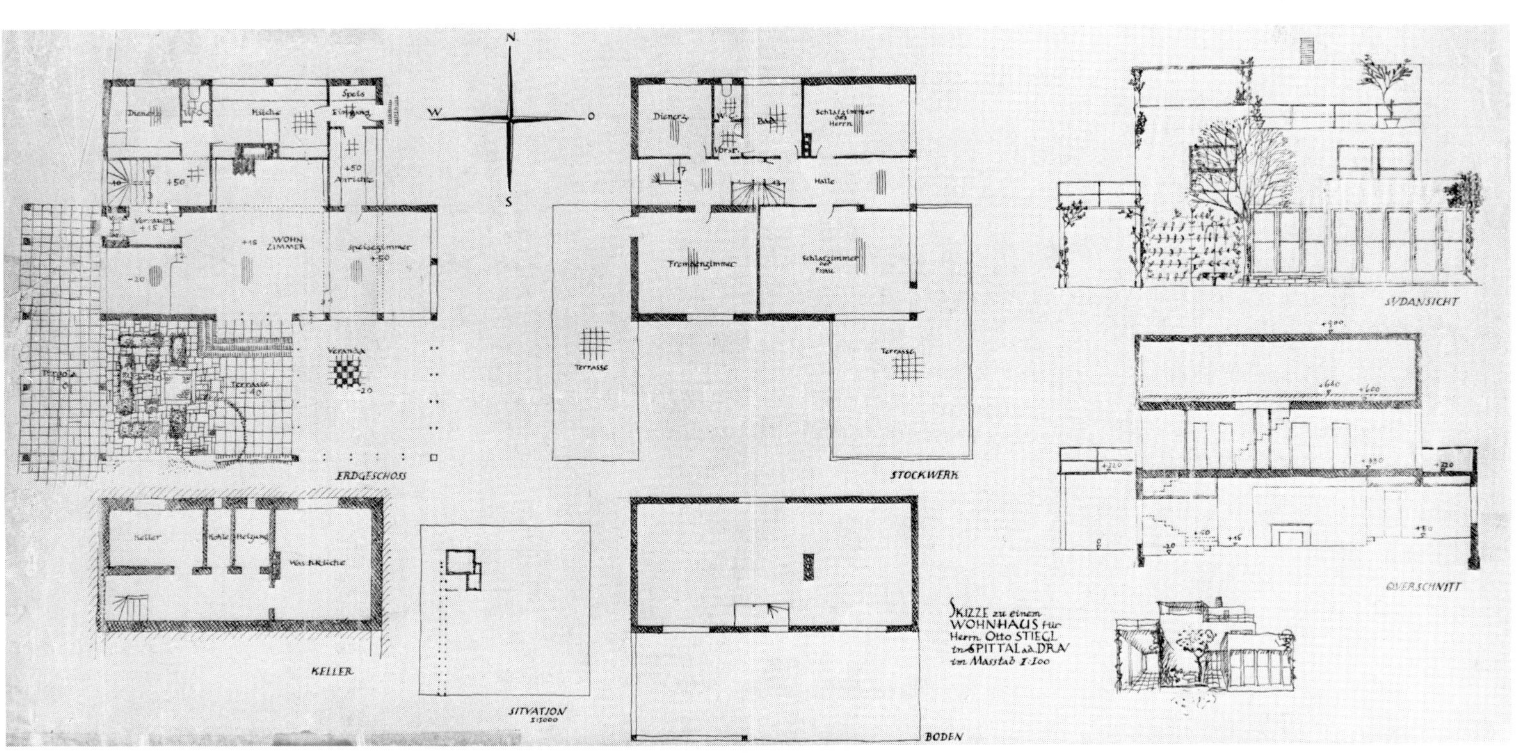

104
Josef Frank
Wohnhaus am Kongreßplatz. Perspektive. Tusche
Residential house at the Kongressplatz. Perspective. Drawing ink

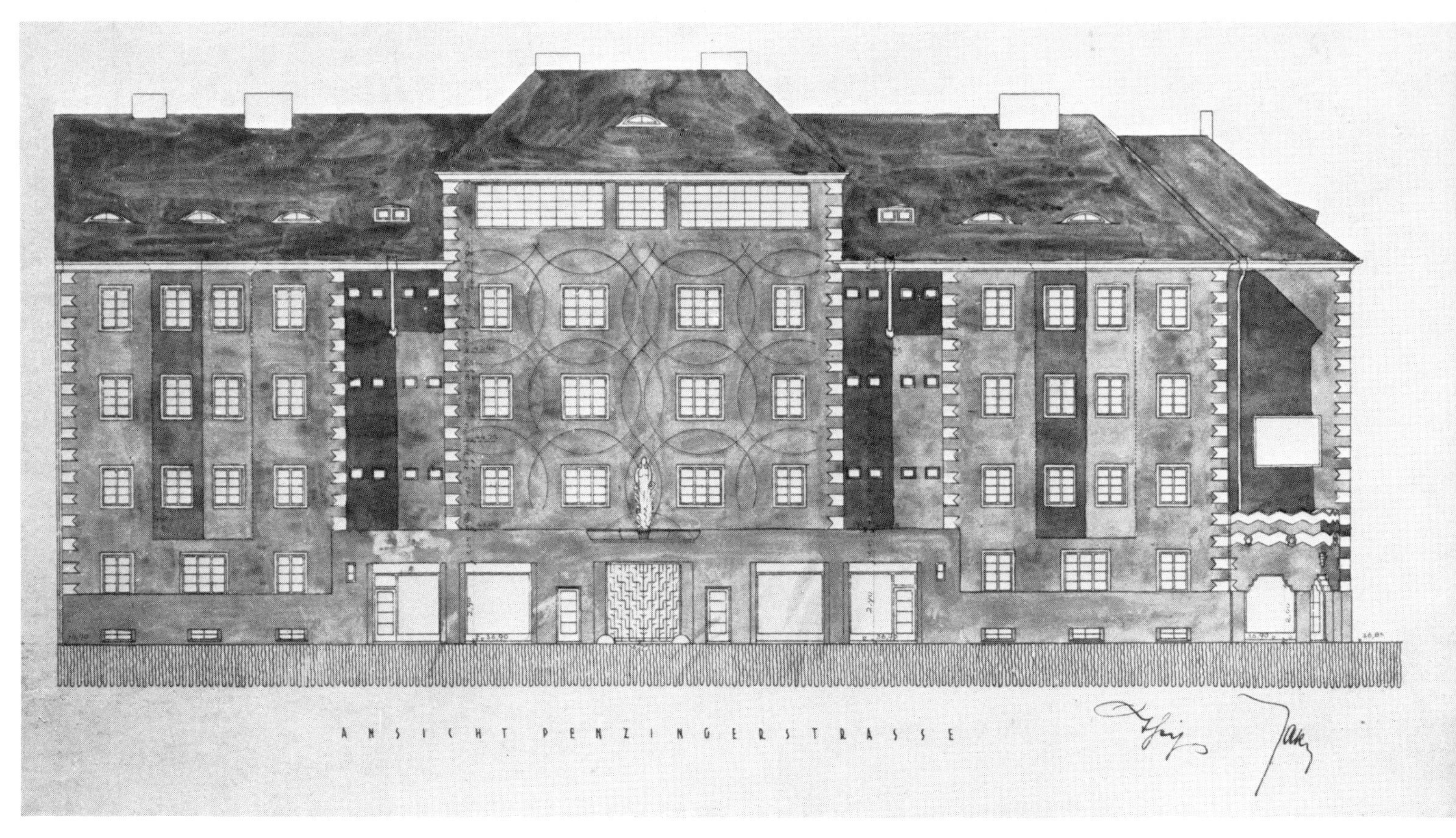

105
Siegfried Theiß/Hans Jaksch
Wohnhausanlage der Gemeinde Wien. Aufriß. Tusche, koloriert
Housing development of the Municipality of Vienna. Elevation. Drawing ink, colored

106
Oswald Haerdtl
Entwurf für eine Kunstschau. Bleistift, Tusche, Aquarellfarbe und Silberpapier
Project for an art show. Pencil, drawing ink, water color and silver paper

107
Oswald Haerdtl
Reihenhaus. Ideenskizze. Bleistift, Tusche und Aquarellfarbe
Terrace house. Concept sketch. Pencil, drawing ink and water color

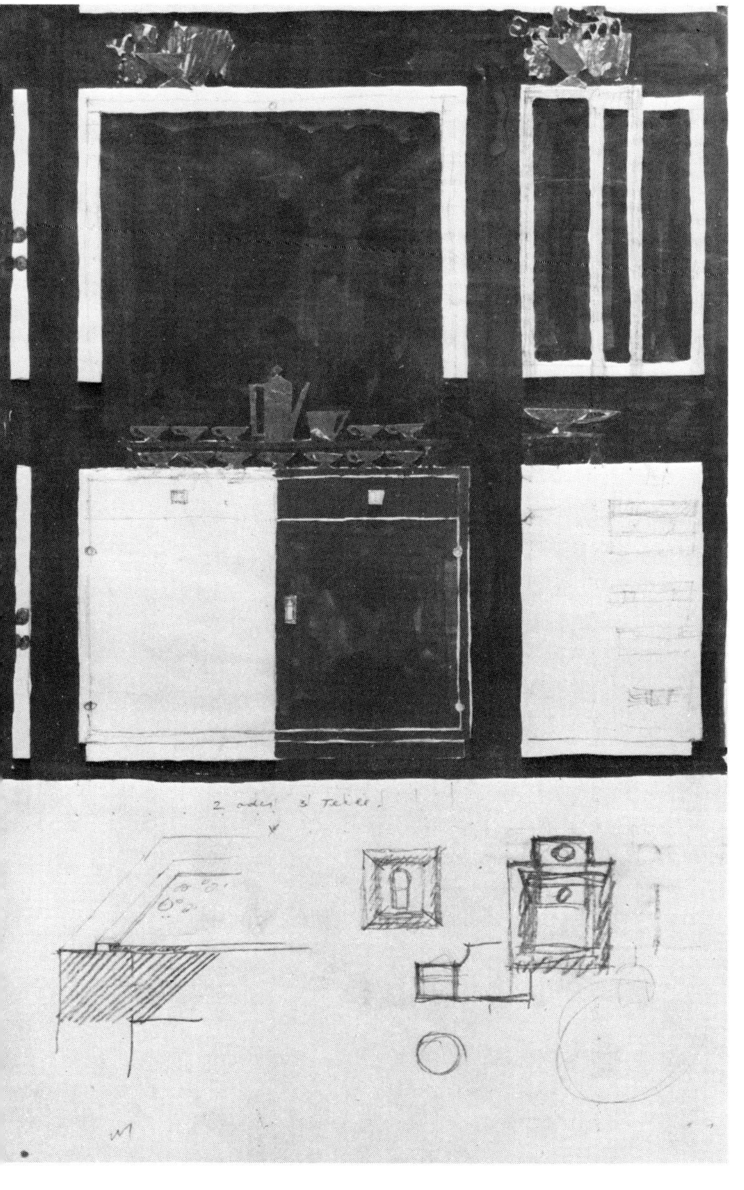

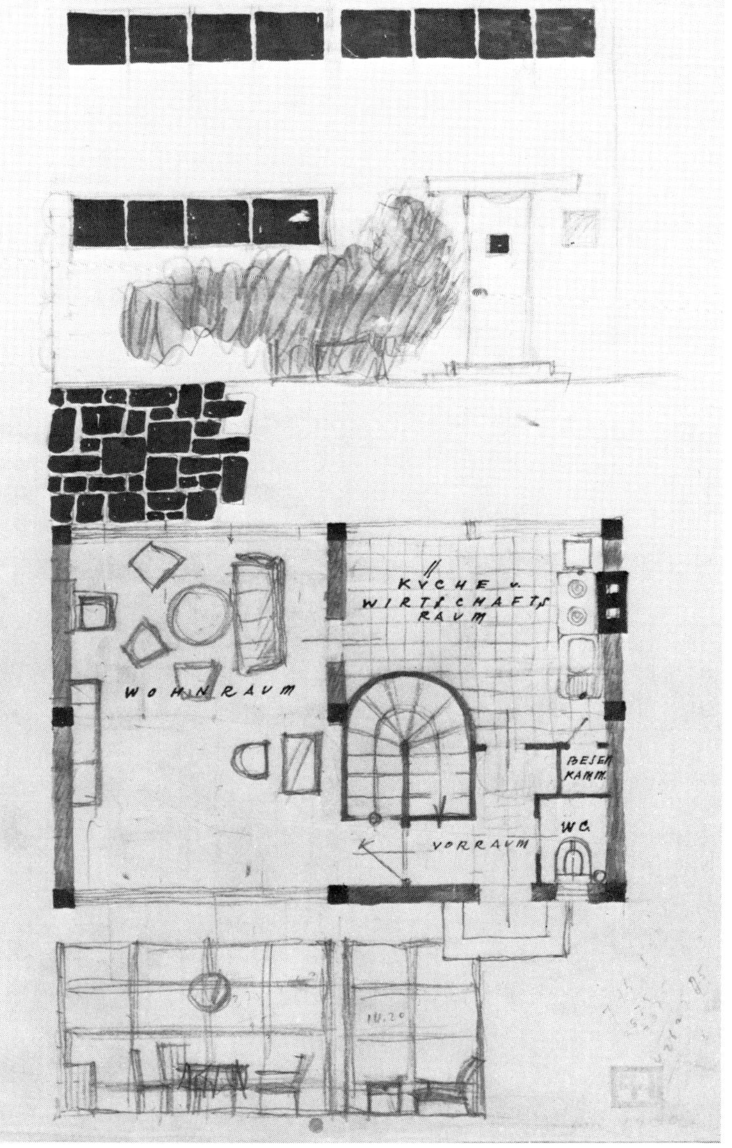

WETTBEWERB FÜR DIE B
BISMARKPLATZES IN
KENNWORT:
„VELDIDENA

108
Clemens Holzmeister
Bebauung des Bismarckplatzes in Innsbruck (Wettbewerbsprojekt). Perspektive. Kohle
Development at the Bismarckplatz in Innsbruck (competition project). Perspective. Charcoal

109
Richard J. Neutra
Waschanstalt in Trebinje. Perspektive. Tinte und Aquarellfarbe
Laundry in Trebinje. Perspective. Ink and water color

Baumann, Ludwig
Born in 1853 in Seibersdorf, Silesia; died in 1936 in Vienna. 1870–74: studied with Gottfried Semper at the Eidgenössisches Polytechnikum in Zurich; 1875–77: employed by Heinrich von Ferstel; 1876–79: architect for the Wienerberger Ziegelfabriks- und Baugesellschaft; from 1896: freelance architect in Vienna; 1888–1929: chief architect of the Kruppsche Metallwarenfabrik in Berndorf; from 1907: principal architect for the Hofburg.
As a representative of Late Historicism, Baumann made a decisive contribution to the unity of the Ringstrasse with buildings such as the war ministry on the Stubenring, begun in 1909.

Ferstel, Heinrich von
Born in 1828 in Vienna; died there in 1883. 1847: attended the Polytechnikum and the school of painting of the Akademie der bildenden Künste in Wien; 1847–50: studied architecture at the Akademie; 1848: Prague; 1859–69: juror and judge of the Viennese Building Commission; from 1866: professor of building design at Vienna's Polytechnisches Institut.
Ferstel, a representative of Historicism, who at the age of 28 was commissioned to build the Neogothic Votivkirche after winning a design competition, was responsible for some of the most important structures of the Ringstrasse era. In addition to the Museum für angewandte Kunst (1868–71), his major late work, the Renaissance-style University (1873–84), must be noted.

Frank, Josef
Born in 1885 in Baden, near Vienna; died in 1967 in Stockholm. 1919–25: professor at Vienna's Kunstgewerbeschule; 1930–32: head of the international Werkbund housing estate in Vienna; 1934: emigrated to Sweden, where he worked for the Svensk Tenn department store.
In Vienna, Frank had a decisive influence on the Austrian architecture of the twenties, at one time in collaboration with Oskar Wlach (furniture store "Haus und Garten"). While in Sweden, he initiated the trend toward simple furnishings of superior craftmanship.

Haerdtl, Oswald
Born in 1899 in Vienna; died there in 1959. Studied with Kolo Moser (painting) and Oskar Strnad (architecture) at Vienna's Kunstgewerbeschule; 1922: joined the office of Josef Hoffmann; 1928: head of Hoffmann's atelier; 1932–38: Hoffmann's partner; 1935: head of a special class for architecture at Vienna's Kunstgewerbeschule; from 1939 on: own workshop; from 1945: leader of a special class for architecture and interior design at the Akademie für angewandte Kunst (formerly Kunstgewerbeschule) in Vienna.
Haerdtl's main activity was in interior decoration. He exerted great influence in this field through his own work, which was distinguished by elegance and superior materials. He also had a strong influence on his students.

Hannich, Josef
Born in 1889 in Vienna; died there in 1962. 1909–12: studied with Otto Wagner at the Akademie der bildenden Künste in Wien. Further data could not be found.
Only a few of Hannich's study works are known.

Hansen, Theophil von
Born in 1813 in Copenhagen; died in 1891 in Vienna. Studied at the Royal Building Academy in Copenhagen; 1840–43: professor at the polytechnical school in Athens; from 1848: member of the Akademie der bildenden Künste in Wien; from 1868: professor there as successor to Eduard van der Nüll.
Hansen was – at a time when this was not as common as today – an "international" architect. In the Vienna of the Ringstrasse era, he found an ideal field for realizing his concept of a Historicism in classical form. With the Heinrichshof (1861–63) he started a new movement in the construction of large residences; he crowned his work with the Parliament Building (1873–83). His influence on architecture and applied arts is noticeable into the twentieth century.

Hasenauer, Carl von
Born in 1833 in Vienna; died there in 1894. 1849–54: studied with Eduard van der Nüll and August Sicard von Siccardsburg at the Akademie der bildenden Künste in Wien; 1854: Akademie prize for architecture; 1861: third prize for the Vienna Opera House; 1884: professor and head of a special school for architecture at the Vienna Akademie.
In his education, his career as well as in his works, Hasenauer was typical of the successful and adaptable architect of the Historicism period. The competition for the Hofmuseen led to a (not always harmonious) working partnership with Gottfried Semper, of which the Hofmuseen (1872–81) and the Burgtheater (1874–88) are some of the products.

Hoffmann, Josef
Born in 1870 in Pirnitz, Moravia; died in 1956 in Vienna. Started his training at the Höhere Staatsgewerbeschule in Brünn; studied at the Akademie der bildenden Künste in Wien, initially with Carl von Hasenauer; from 1894: with Otto Wagner; won the Rome prize; from 1896: employed in the atelier of Otto Wagner; 1897: cofounder of the Viennese Secession; 1898–1936: professor of architecture at Vienna's Kunstgewerbeschule and head of various workshops (enamel, metal); 1903: establishment of the Wiener Werkstätte; 1912: founding member of the Austrian Werkbund; president of the Viennese Secession.
After training under Otto Wagner, Hoffmann's development was influenced first by the flowery Art Nouveau style and subsequently by the rigid one of Charles Rennie Mackintosh. With his best works – Purkersdorf Sanatorium (1904–06), Palais Stoclet in Brussels (1905–11) – he had a profound stylistic influence throughout Europe.

Holzmeister, Clemens
Born in 1886 in Fulpmes, the Tyrol. Studied at the Technische Hochschule Wien; 1914–19: assistant, doctorate in 1919; 1924–38: professor and head of a master class at the Akademie der bildenden Künste in Wien; 1928–32: also professor at the Kunstakademie in Düsseldorf; 1940–49: professor at the college of technology in Istanbul; 1954–57: once more professor at the Akademie in Vienna.
An artist as versatile as he is prolific, Holzmeister is very Austrian in his basic "baroqueness." Next to his projects in Ankara, church buildings have always ranked high in his work, and several of them are ranked among the most remarkable accomplishments in this field.

Hoppe, Emil
Born in 1876 in Vienna; died in 1957 in Salzburg. 1898–1901: studied with Otto Wagner at the Akademie der bildenden Künste in Wien.
(For further information, see Schönthal.)

Jaksch, Hans
Born in 1879 near Reichenberg; died in 1970 in Vienna. Started his training at the Staatsgewerbeschule in Vienna; later, studied at the Technische Hochschule Wien; freelance architect in a working partnership with Siegfried Theiß; 1952: was given the title of professor.
(For further information, see Theiß.)

Kammerer, Marcel
Born in 1878 in Vienna; died in 1959 in Quebec. Started his training with Camillo Sitte at the Staatsgewerbeschule in Vienna; 1898–1901: studied with Otto Wagner at the Akademie der bildenden Künste in Wien; until 1910: employed in the atelier of Otto Wagner; after 1910: freelance architect, at one time in collaboration with Emil Hoppe and Otto Schönthal.
As the leading draftsman after Joseph Maria Olbrich in Otto Wagner's workshop, Kammerer put great value on graphic presentation and, moreover, considered himself a painter.

Kaym, Franz
Born in 1891 in Moosbrunn, near Vienna; died in 1949 in Vienna. 1910–13: studied with Otto Wagner at the Akademie der bildenden Künste in Wien; member of the Wiener Künstlerhaus; collaborated with another Wagner student, Alfons Hetmanek.
The economic conditions of the interwar period prevented Kaym, like so many in his age group, from securing larger contracts. His main field of activity was in Vienna's communal housing development.

Loos, Adolf
Born in 1870 in Brünn; died in 1933 in Kalksburg, near Vienna. 1887/88: attended the Staatsgewerbeschule in Reichenberg; 1890–93: studied at the Technische Hochschule Dresden; 1893–96: resided in America; 1912–14: ran his own school of architecture; 1920–22: chief architect of the housing department of the Municipality of Vienna; 1922–27: resided in France; 1928: returned to Vienna.
Loos was the most consequent of all Austrian architects at the beginning of the twentieth century; his fanatical striving for honesty brought him in conflict with his contemporaries and with their conceptions of form. Even more than with his buildings – several of which (for example the Goldman & Salatsch House in the Michaelerplatz, Vienna) made architectural history – he influenced the architects who succeeded him with his writings *(Ins Leere gesprochen; Trotzdem)*.

Neutra, Richard J.
Born in 1892 in Vienna; died in 1970 in Wuppertal. Studied at the Technische Hochschule Wien; 1922: assistant to Erich Mendelsohn in Berlin; 1924: emigrated to the USA; worked in

Frank Lloyd Wright's atelier; from 1926: had his own atelier in Los Angeles.
For Neutra's work, the emigration to America at a relatively early age was the big turning-point which paved the way for a completely different development from that of his colleagues in Vienna. Neutra's particular merit lies in his attempts to put ecological and biological findings to use in architecture.

Nüll, Eduard van der
Born in 1812 in Vienna; died there in 1886. Studied at the Akademie der bildenden Künste in Wien; 1839–43: traveled to Italy and France (together with August Sicard von Siccardsburg); spent some time in Germany; from 1844: professor of architecture and ornamentation at the Vienna Akademie; working partnership with August Sicard von Siccardsburg.
(For further information, see Sicard von Siccardsburg.)

Ohmann, Friedrich
Born in 1858 in Lemberg; died in 1927 in Vienna. Studied at the Technische Hochschule Wien and the Akademie der bildenden Künste in Wien; assistant at the Technische Hochschule Wien; teacher at the Staatsgewerbeschule in Vienna; 1889–99: professor of architecture at the Kunstgewerbeschule in Prague; 1899–1907: principal architect for the Hofburg in Vienna; 1904–23: professor and head of a master class at the Vienna Akademie.
Ohmann remained true to Historicism in his work, although components reminiscent of Art Nouveau were sometimes visible. He is considered one of the best draftsmen of his generation.

Olbrich, Joseph Maria
Born in 1867 in Troppau; died in 1908 in Düsseldorf. Studied with Carl von Hasenauer and Otto Wagner at the Akademie der bildenden Künste in Wien; won a Rome prize; 1894: returned to Vienna following various travels; until 1898: worked in the atelier of Otto Wagner; 1897: cofounder of the Viennese Secession; 1899: appointment to the Darmstadt Künstlerkolonie.
In Vienna, Olbrich's name is linked inseparably with the Secession, as the architect of the building itself and as a cofounder of the movement. The first real opportunity to develop his architectural capabilities came to him in Darmstadt, where he paved the way for important developments right up to industrial manufacture.

Plečnik, Josef
Born in 1872 in Ljubljana; died there in 1957. 1895–98: studied with Otto Wagner at the Akademie der bildenden Künste in Wien; 1910–20: teacher at the Kunstgewerbeschule in Prague; 1920: appointment to a professorship at the faculty of technology of Ljubljana University.
Considered one of Wagner's most remarkable students, Plečnik nevertheless continued to develop his architectonic talents independently. His influence is especially noticeable in his hometown, where the effect on his students is still felt to the present day.

Schönthal, Otto
Born in 1878 in Vienna; died there in 1961. 1896–1909: employed in the atelier of Otto Wagner; 1898–1901 studied with Otto Wagner at the Akademie der bildenden Künste in Wien; from 1909: freelance architect together with Emil Hoppe; 1911–14: also collaborated with Marcel Kammerer; 1918–38: had a working partnership with Emil Hoppe.
Hoppe and Schönthal too are indebted to their teacher, Otto Wagner, for the basis of their work, although historicized elements can sometimes be seen in it. Their most significant accomplishments were in the field of communal housing development during the period between the wars.

Semper, Gottfried
Born in 1803 in Hamburg; died in 1879 in Rome. First studied mathematics at the University of Göttingen; later, began architectural studies at the Akademie der bildenden Künste in Munich; 1826–27 and 1829–30: traveled and stayed in Paris; 1834: appointment to the Bauakademie in Dresden; participated in the construction of barricades in Dresden during the revolt of 1849; until 1851: in Paris; 1851–55: lived in London; 1855: appointed to the Eidgenössisches Polytechnikum in Zurich; 1871–76: worked in Vienna, by appointment of Emperor Franz Joseph.
Semper already had an international career behind him when he was called to Vienna by the emperor as a consultant to review Hasenauer's plans for the Hofmuseen. Of great significance are his theoretical writings, in which he was an early proponent of the proper use of building materials, thus becoming one of the pioneers of modern architecture.

Sicard von Siccardsburg, August
Born in 1813 in Budapest; died in 1868 in Vienna. Studied in Vienna; 1839–43: traveled; from 1843: professor of architecture at the Akademie der bildenden Künste in Wien; 1865–67: head of a special class; working partnership with Eduard van der Nüll.
Sicard von Siccardsburg and Eduard van der Nüll are generally mentioned together: both were about the same age, had been friends since their youth and later formed a partnership, of which several buildings characteristic of the Historicism period in Vienna are products. Sicard von Siccardsburg was mainly responsible for technical and business matters, while van der Nüll undertook the design and artistic work. Their main achievement is the Opera House (1861–69), whose completion neither lived to see.

Strnad, Oskar
Born in 1879 in Vienna; died in 1935 in Bad Aussee, Styria. Studied at the Technische Hochschule Wien, and got his doctorate in 1904; following study trips, was employed in the atelier of Friedrich Ohmann; from 1909: leader of the class in general studies of form at Vienna's Kunstgewerbeschule; from 1912: professor; from 1914: head of a special class for architecture; from 1918: in charge of the Tessenow class as well; since 1919: also worked as a stage designer.
Strnad must be regarded above all as an eminent teacher who grounded his teaching in philosophical principles. His drawings show him to be an aquarellist of great individuality, whence his connection to stage design.

Theiß, Siegfried
Born in 1882 in Bratislava; died in 1963 in Vienna. Studied at the Technische Hochschule Wien and, as a master student of Friedrich Ohmann, at the Akademie der bildenden Künste in Wien; from 1907: freelance architect in partnership with Hans Jaksch; 1919–24: associate professor; from 1924: full professor at the Technische Hochschule Wien.
Together with Hans Jaksch, Theiß ran one of the most significant workshops of the interwar period, where, among other things, the first high-rise building in Vienna was designed, and where important contributions were made to the communal housing development.

Wagner, Otto
Born in 1841 in Penzing, near Vienna; died in 1918 in Vienna. 1857–59: attended the Polytechnisches Institut in Vienna; 1860–61: studied at the Königliche Bauakademie in Berlin; 1861–63: studied with August Sicard von Siccardsburg and Eduard van der Nüll at the Akademie der bildenden Künste in Wien; from 1884: artistic advisor to the Commission for Viennese Traffic Facilities; 1894–1912: professor and head of a special class at the Vienna Akademie as successor of Carl von Hasenauer; 1913–15: continued teaching as honorary professor; 1899–1905: member of the Viennese Secession.
Wagner is the most important Viennese architect of the late nineteenth and early twentieth centuries. An exponent of Historicism in his initial period of work, he later broke away from the classical patterns, especially in the formal field, and with new materials built simple structures with unobtrusive surface ornamentation. His pioneer work in Vienna is the Postal Savings Bank. Through his buildings and through his gifted students, he led modern Austrian architecture to a high point which has remained unequalled. His expertise in design and attention to detail can be noted in his drawings.

1. Theophil von Hansen. Herrenhaus (Upper Chamber). Elevation of the main façade. 1865. Signed Hansen. Drawing ink. 47,5×94,5 cm. Akademie der bildenden Künste in Wien (19797).
2. Theophil von Hansen. Herrenhaus. Elevation of the main façade. 1865. Pencil and water color. 18,5×35 cm. Akademie der bildenden Künste in Wien (19794).
3. Theophil von Hansen. Herrenhaus. Section. 1865. Signed Hansen. Black and colored drawing ink. 47,5×94,5 cm. Akademie der bildenden Künste in Wien (19792).
4. Theophil von Hansen. Parliament. Elevation sketch of the lateral façade. 1870. Drawing ink. 10,4×29 cm. Akademie der bildenden Künste in Wien (20862b).
5. Theophil von Hansen. Parliament. Elevation sketch of the main façade. 1870. Signed Hansen. Drawing ink. 10×39,6 cm. Akademie der bildenden Künste in Wien (20862a).
6. Theophil von Hansen. Parliament. Perspective sketch. 1887. Signed Hansen. Pencil and chalk. 31×62 cm. Akademie der bildenden Künste in Wien (20863).
7. Heinrich von Ferstel. University (first design). Elevation of the main façade. 1871. Signed Ferstel. Drawing ink and water color. 58,4×76,9 cm. Historisches Museum der Stadt Wien (F VIII a/9).
8. Heinrich von Ferstel. University. Elevations and plan of the projecting center. 1871. Pencil. 56,5×47,5 cm. Historisches Museum der Stadt Wien (F VIII d/3).
9. Heinrich von Ferstel. Wertheim Residence, Schwarzenbergplatz. Elevation of the main façade. Drawing ink. 58×84,4 cm. Historisches Museum der Stadt Wien (F XXIII/38).
10. Gottfried Semper and Carl von Hasenauer. Structure linking the Hofburg with the museums. Bird's-eye view. 1869. Signed Semper, Hasenauer. Black and brown drawing ink. 43×63 cm. Haus-, Hof- und Staatsarchiv, Vienna, Planarchiv Burghauptmannschaft (portfolio D 4).
11. Gottfried Semper and Carl von Hasenauer. Extension of the Hofburg in connection with the new construction of the museums and of the Hofburgtheater. Elevation and section. 1871. Signed Semper, Hasenauer. Drawing ink with brown wash. 34,5×176 cm. Haus-, Hof- und Staatsarchiv, Vienna, Planarchiv Burghauptmannschaft (large format).
12. Gottfried Semper and Carl von Hasenauer. Hofschauspielhaus. Plan of the box level. Before 1874. Signed Semper, Hasenauer. Drawing ink. 40,6×64 cm. Graphische Sammlung Albertina, Vienna (19/6/63–8657).
13. Gottfried Semper and Carl von Hasenauer. Hofschauspielhaus. Elevation of a part of the lateral façade. 1873. Signed Semper, Hasenauer. Drawing ink. 51,5×69 cm. Graphische Sammlung Albertina, Vienna (19/6/72–8665).
14. August Sicard von Siccardsburg and Eduard van der Nüll. Opera. Elevation of the main façade. Before 1863. With monogram A.S.E.N. Drawing ink. 56,4×143,5 cm. Graphische Sammlung Albertina, Vienna (GM 4701, 64).
15. Ludwig Baumann. Rudolf von Habsburg Monument. Perspective sketch. 1907. Pencil. 26,5×44,5 cm. Haus-, Hof- und Staatsarchiv, Vienna, Planarchiv Burghauptmannschaft (portfolio D 10).
16. Ludwig Baumann. Hofburg. Elevation of a wall in the parterre hall. 1914. Pencil, drawing ink and water color. 41×107 cm. Haus-, Hof- und Staatsarchiv, Vienna, Planarchiv Burghauptmannschaft (large format).
17. Friedrich Ohmann. Insurance building in Prague. Perspective sketch. 1894. Signed Ohmann. Sepia with wash. 23,7×18,5 cm. Wilhelmine Pfann-Ohmann.
18. Friedrich Ohmann. Palm house. Perspective sketch. 1901. Drawing ink with wash, pencil and crayon. 35×67 cm. Wilhelmine Pfann-Ohmann.
19. Friedrich Ohmann. Radetzkybrücke. Perspective. Around 1901. Drawing ink and water color. 40,5×57,4 cm. Historisches Museum der Stadt Wien (106.931).
20. Friedrich Ohmann. Hofburg. Section. 1905. Drawing ink, pencil and crayon. 32,5×52 cm. Wilhelmine Pfann-Ohmann.
21. Friedrich Ohmann. Hofburg. Perspective section through the staircase. 1905. Pencil. 56,3×40 cm. Wilhelmine Pfann-Ohmann.
22. Friedrich Ohmann. Kaiserin Elisabeth Monument. Elevation sketch of the planting. 1905. Drawing ink, pencil and crayon. 9,8×53 cm. Historisches Museum der Stadt Wien (106.884/1).
23. Friedrich Ohmann. Kaiserin Elisabeth Monument. Elevation sketch. 1905. Drawing ink, water color and pastel chalk. 12,2×38,8 cm. Historisches Museum der Stadt Wien (106.883/1).
24. Friedrich Ohmann and Josef Hackhofer. Mouth of the Wienfluß in the Stadtpark. Perspective. 1906. Drawing ink and water color. 69×115 cm. Historisches Museum der Stadt Wien (93.306).
25. Friedrich Ohmann. Dianabad. Perspective. 1912. Drawing ink and pencil, heightened with white. 56,3×60 cm. Wilhelmine Pfann-Ohmann.
26. Otto Wagner. Palace of Justice. Elevation of the lateral façade. 1874. Signed Wagner. Drawing ink and water color. 67×85 cm. Graphische Sammlung Albertina, Vienna (26/2/12/8126).
27. Otto Wagner. Palace of Justice. Section. 1874. Signed Wagner. Drawing ink and water color. 67×85 cm. Graphische Sammlung Albertina, Vienna (26/2/12/8128).
28. Otto Wagner. Kapuzinerkirche with imperial tomb (reconstruction study). Perspective. 1898. Drawing ink with wash, heightened with white. 41×52,7 cm. Graphische Sammlung Albertina, Vienna (29/3a/2/9744).
29. Otto Wagner. Court Pavilion of the Hietzing city railway station. Elevation. 1896. Drawing ink and water color, heightened with white. 45,5×70 cm. Graphische Sammlung Albertina, Vienna (43/3/2/9658).
30. Otto Wagner. Karlsplatz city railway station. Perspectives and ground plan detail. 1898. Drawing ink and water color. 65×46 cm. Historisches Museum der Stadt Wien (77.262).
31. Otto Wagner. Akademie der bildenden Künste. Bird's-eye view. 1898. Drawing ink and water color, lettering heightened with gold. 40×45,7 cm. Historisches Museum der Stadt Wien (96.015/19).
32. Otto Wagner. Art gallery. Elevation sketch of the main façade. Pencil and yellow crayon. 34,5×50 cm. Privately owned.
33. Otto Wagner. Galerie für Werke der Kunst unserer Zeit. Elevation of the main façade. 1900. Drawing ink and water color. 34,5×88,3 cm. Historisches Museum der Stadt Wien (146.208).
34. Otto Wagner. Kaiser-Franz-Joseph-Stadtmuseum (project for the open competition). Perspective. 1901. Drawing ink and crayon. 36,7×51,8 cm. Historisches Museum der Stadt Wien (96.049).
35. Otto Wagner. International art exhibition in Vienna. Elevation of the lateral façade and section 1903. Drawing ink and water color. 20,9×41,9 cm. Akademie der bildenden Künste in Wien (22515).
36. Otto Wagner. International art exhibition in Vienna. Elevation of the main façade. 1903. Drawing ink and water color. 20,9×41,9 cm. Akademie der bildenden Künste in Wien (22516).
37. Otto Wagner. International art exhibition in Vienna. Ground plan. 1903. Drawing ink and water color. 20,9×41,9 cm. Akademie der bildenden Künste in Wien (22518).
38. Otto Wagner. Postal Savings Bank. Elevation of the main façade. Around 1906. Drawing ink. 54,5×135 cm. Österreichische Postsparkasse, Vienna.
39. Otto Wagner. Postal Savings Bank. Working drawing. Before 1904. Drawing ink and water color. 255×102 cm. Österreichische Postsparkasse, Vienna.
40. Otto Wagner. Detail from illustration 39.
41. Otto Wagner. Jubilee Fountain at the Karlsplatz. Perspective elevation. 1903. Pencil, heightened with white. 33,8×29,5 cm. Historisches Museum der Stadt Wien (96.281).
42. Otto Wagner. Karlsplatz with Jubilee Fountain Perspective. 1903. Pencil and zinc white. 26,7×53,7 cm. Historisches Museum der Stadt Wien (96.006/22).
43. Otto Wagner. Kirche Am Steinhof. Perspective sketch. 1902. Pencil, water color and gold paint. 32,3×26,3 cm. Historisches Museum der Stadt Wien (96.011/1).
44. Otto Wagner. Kirche Am Steinhof. Perspective. 1902. Drawing ink and water color. 59×50,2 cm. Historisches Museum der Stadt Wien (96.011/2).
45. Otto Wagner. Kirche Am Steinhof. Elevation of the main façade. 1903/04. Drawing ink. 67,8×48,8 cm. Historisches Museum der Stadt Wien (96.011/15).
46. Otto Wagner. Kirche Am Steinhof. Perspective elevation of the high altar. 1903/04. Drawing ink and pencil. 62,8×46,8 cm. Historisches Museum der Stadt Wien (96.011/3).
47. Otto Wagner. Temporary church. Perspective sketch. 1905. Pencil and crayon. 36,5×25,4 cm. Privately owned.
48. Otto Wagner. Temporary church. Perspective sketch. 1905. Pencil and crayon. 34,5×31 cm. Privately owned.
49. Otto Wagner. Temporary church. Perspective sketch of the interior. 1905. Pencil and crayon. 35×31 cm. Privately owned.
50. Otto Wagner. Temporary church. Perspective sketch of the interior. 1905. Pencil and crayon. 20,2×37,2 cm. Privately owned.
51. Otto Wagner. Villa Wagner. Perspective and ground plan. 1905. Drawing ink and water color. 56,5×46,3 cm. Historisches Museum der Stadt Wien (95.003/1).
52. Otto Wagner. Tenement house, Neustiftgasse 40. Perspective. 1909. Drawing ink. 40,5×22,1 cm. Historisches Museum der Stadt Wien (96.010/1).
53. Otto Wagner. Kaiser-Franz-Joseph-Stadtmuseum at the Karlsplatz (third project). Perspective sketch. 1909. Pencil and drawing ink, heightened with white. 12,5×17,8 cm. Akademie der bildenden Künste in Wien (26684).
54. Otto Wagner. Hotel at the Karlsplatz. Perspective. 1910/11. Drawing ink, pencil and water color. 34,1×48 cm. Historisches Museum der Stadt Wien (57.114/1).

5. Otto Wagner. Ideal design of the 22nd district. 3ird's-eye view. 1910/11. Drawing ink. 1×82 cm. Historisches Museum der Stadt Wien 96.022).
6. Otto Wagner. Kaiser-Franz-Joseph-Stadt- nuseum auf der Schmelz. Perspective. 912. Drawing ink, heightened with white. 5×75,5 cm. Historisches Museum der Stadt Wien (56.937).
7. Otto Wagner. Exhibition halls. Perspective sketch. 1912. Pencil. 14,5×21,3 cm. Privately owned.
8. Otto Wagner. Sankt-Magdalenen-Spital. Elevation of a part of the façade. Pencil and drawing ink, colored and heightened with white. 4×76,5 cm. Privately owned.
9. Otto Wagner. Kaiser-Franz-Josephs- Stiftungs-Lazarett. Perspective. Drawing ink. 9,5×67 cm. Privately owned.
0. Joseph Maria Olbrich. Theater project. Perspective. 1893. Signed Olbrich. Drawing ink, pencil and water color, heightened with white. 9,7×52,4 cm. Kunstbibliothek Berlin (10020).
1. Joseph Maria Olbrich. Franzensbrücke. Perspective sketch with drawn passepartout. 896. Drawing ink with wash and water color. ,8×13,9 cm. Kunstbibliothek Berlin (10066).
2. Joseph Maria Olbrich. Secession exhibition building. Perspective sketch of the main entrance. 897/98. Signed Olbrich. Pencil, drawing ink, water color and poster paint. 18,7×11,6 cm. Kunstbibliothek Berlin (10070).
3. Joseph Maria Olbrich. Secession exhibition building. Elevation sketch of the main façade. 897/98. Signed Olbrich. Drawing ink with wash nd water color, heightened with gold. 1,1×21,1 cm. Kunstbibliothek Berlin (10084).
4. Joseph Maria Olbrich. Secession exhibition building. Elevation of the main façade. Signature Gustav Klimt Präsident." Signed Olbrich. Drawing ink and water color. 59,7×47 cm. Wiener Secession.
5. Joseph Maria Olbrich. Jubilee Pavilion of the City of Vienna. Elevation and perspective sketches f the main façade. 1897. Drawing ink and pencil. 3×19,6 cm. Kunstbibliothek Berlin (10092).
6. Joseph Maria Olbrich. Station building of the iennese city railway (?). Perspective sketch. 897/98. Drawing ink. 16,4×23,3 cm. Kunstbibliothek Berlin (10069).
7. Joseph Maria Olbrich. Pavilion of the Radfahr- lub der Staats- und Hofbeamten (Civil Servants' nd Court Officials' Cycling Club). Elevation, round plan, section. 1898. Drawing ink, pencil nd water color. 36,5×51 cm. Wiener Secession.
8. Joseph Maria Olbrich. Pavilion of the adfahrclub der Staats- und Hofbeamten. erspective elevation of the main façade. 1898. igned Olbrich. Drawing ink, pencil and water olor. 17,5×20 cm. Wiener Secession.
9. Joseph Maria Olbrich. Secession exhibition uilding. Perspective. 1897. Drawing ink and ater color. Drawing 12,4×9,6 cm (size of sheet 5×50 cm). Historisches Museum der Stadt Wien 93.308/1).
0. Josef Plečnik. Residence. Perspective. 1898. igned Plečnik. Pencil and blue ink. 5,7×21,4 cm. Arhitekturni Muzej Ljubljana.
1. Josef Plečnik. Palace. Perspective sketch. round 1900. Green ink and crayon. 1,2×22,2 cm. Arhitekturni Muzej Ljubljana.
2. Josev Plečnik. Façade study. Around 902–04. Drawing ink. 26,2×14,8 cm. Arhitekturni uzej Ljubljana.
73. Josef Plečnik. Residence. Elevation of the entrance façade and ground plan. 1908. Drawing ink and water color, cut out and stuck onto red paper. 21,5×24 cm. Arhitekturni Muzej Ljubljana.
74. Josef Hannich. Tenement house, Wiednerhauptstrasse (student project under Otto Wagner). Elevation. 1910. Pencil and drawing ink, colored. 33,5×27 cm. Privately owned.
75. Josef Hannich. Tenement house, Wiednerhauptstrasse (student project under Otto Wagner). Perspective. 1910. Pencil and drawing ink, colored. 39×21,7 cm. Privately owned.
76. Josef Hannich. Group of houses in Weidling (student project under Otto Wagner). Bird's-eye view. 1911. Drawing ink and pencil. 35,5×35,5 cm. Privately owned.
77. Josef Hannich. House in the Auhofstrasse (student project under Otto Wagner). Bird's-eye view. 1911. Drawing ink, pencil and crayon. 37,5×45 cm. Privately owned.
78. Josef Hannich. Extension of the Vienna Hofburg (student project under Otto Wagner). Perspective. 1912. Pencil, drawing ink and zinc white. 44,5×81,5 cm. Privately owned.
79. Franz Kaym. Monastery (student project in the honorary year of Otto Wagner at the Akademie). Perspective and ground plan. 1911/12. Signed Kaym. Pencil, drawing ink and water color. 31,6×28,8 cm. Privately owned.
80. Franz Kaym. Country church (student project in the honorary year of Otto Wagner at the Akademie). Perspective and ground plan. 1911/12. Pencil, crayon, drawing ink and gold paint, heightened with white. 14×14 cm. Privately owned.
81. Otto Schönthal. Residence. Perspective. Signed Schönthal. Pencil and water color. 23×36 cm. Privately owned.
82. Emil Hoppe, Marcel Kammerer and Otto Schönthal. Theater hall. Perspective. 1916. Pencil and water color. 32,8×31 cm. Privately owned.
83. Adolf Loos. Fireplace niche. Perspective sketch. Around 1899. Pencil. 27,2×42 cm. Graphische Sammlung Albertina, Vienna (0707 A 8).
84. Adolf Loos. Interior. Perspective sketch. 1899. Drawing ink and crayon. 19,8×22,4 cm. Graphische Sammlung Albertina, Vienna (00108 D 3).
85. Adolf Loos. Building in the Stadtpark area. Perspective sketch. Around 1907. Pencil. 27,2×14 cm. Graphische Sammlung Albertina, Vienna (0682 F 10).
86. Adolf Loos. Monument to Kaiser Franz Joseph. Elevation sketch. Around 1917. Pencil. 34×21 cm. Graphische Sammlung Albertina, Vienna (0435 C 2).
87. Josef Hoffmann. Bed. Perspective. Drawing ink. 18,5×17,9 cm. Österreichisches Museum für angewandte Kunst, Vienna (XXII h/26).
88. Josef Hoffmann. Purkersdorf Sanatorium. Ground plan sketch. Before 1904. Drawing ink, pencil and crayon. 21×34 cm. Johannes Spalt.
89. Josef Hoffmann. Purkersdorf Sanatorium. Elevation sketch. Before 1904. Drawing ink and pencil. 21×34 cm. Johannes Spalt.
90. Josef Hoffmann. Chairs. Elevation sketches. 1904. Drawing ink, pencil and crayon. 20,6×34 cm. Österreichisches Museum für angewandte Kunst, Vienna (XXII h/1).
91. Josef Hoffmann. Table with mirror and stool. Concept sketch. Signed Hoffmann. Pencil. 21×34 cm. Johannes Spalt.
92. Josef Hoffmann. Knips House. Elevation sketch of the entrance façade. Before 1923. Drawing ink. 17×45,4 cm. Österreichisches Museum für angewandte Kunst, Vienna (XXII h/24).
93. Josef Hoffmann. Klosehof. Elevation sketch. Before 1924. Drawing ink. 20,8×33,4 cm. Österreichisches Museum für angewandte Kunst, Vienna (XXII h/4).
94. Josef Hoffmann. High-rise building. Elevation sketch. 1927. Signed Hoffmann. Pencil. 20,5×16,8 cm. Österreichisches Museum für angewandte Kunst, Vienna (XXII h/9).
95. Josef Hoffmann. Residential house. Elevation sketch. Signed Hoffmann. Pencil, drawing ink and water color. 31×20,5 cm. Privately owned.
96. Josef Hoffmann. Residential house for the Municipality of Vienna. Elevation sketch. 1929. Signed Hoffmann. Pencil. 20,5×34,1 cm. Österreichisches Museum für angewandte Kunst, Vienna (XXII h/18).
97. Josef Hoffmann. House for the Werkbund housing estate. Elevation sketches. Before 1930. Signed Hoffmann. Pencil and crayon. 21×34,3 cm. Österreichisches Museum für angewandte Kunst, Vienna (XXII h/12).
98. Josef Hoffmann. Exhibition hall of the Wiener Werkstätten. Sketch of ground floor and elevation. 1929. Signed Hoffmann. Ink. 42,2×33 cm. Akademie der bildenden Künste in Wien (26298).
99. Josef Hoffmann. Garden pavilion. Elevation sketch. Ink. 21×22 cm. Privately owned.
100. Oskar Strnad. War Ministry (competition project). Perspective. 1908. Signed Strnad. Drawing ink and water color. 56,6×38,7 cm. Österreichisches Museum für angewandte Kunst, Vienna (KJ 13892/2).
101. Oskar Strnad. Projections of walls. Signed Strnad. Drawing ink. 32,3×42 cm. Österreichisches Museum für angewandte Kunst, Vienna (KJ 13871/10).
102. Josef Frank. Traiskirchen housing estate. Site plan ot the estate and plans of a terrace house (floor plans, elevation and section). Around 1921. Signed Frank. Drawing ink. 36,5×25 cm. Graphische Sammlung Albertina, Vienna (Frank-Archiv).
103. Josef Frank. Residence in Spittal/Drau. Sketch of site, floor plans, section, elevation and perspective. Drawing ink. 30×64 cm. Graphische Sammlung Albertina, Vienna (Frank-Archiv).
104. Josef Frank. Residential house at the Kongressplatz. Perspective. 1923. Signed Frank. Drawing ink. 32×41,6 cm. Graphische Sammlung Albertina, Vienna (Frank-Archiv).
105. Siegfried Theiß and Hans Jaksch. Housing development of the Municipality of Vienna. Elevation. Before 1924. Signed Theiß, Jaksch. Drawing ink, colored. 33×54 cm. Walter Jaksch.
106. Oswald Haerdtl. Project for an art show. 1927. Pencil, drawing ink, water color and silver paper. 34×21 cm. Carmela Haerdtl.
107. Oswald Haerdtl. Terrace house. Concept sketch. 1930. Pencil, drawing ink and water color. 34×21 cm. Carmela Haerdtl.
108. Clemens Holzmeister. Development at the Bismarckplatz in Innsbruck (competition project). Perspective. 1922. Charcoal. 37,3×51,5 cm. Graphische Sammlung Albertina, Vienna (Holzmeister-Archiv).
109. Richard J. Neutra. Laundry in Trebinje. Perspective. 1915. Ink and water color. 14,2×25,6 cm. Dione Neutra.

Sources of quotations

[1] Gottfried Semper, from the introduction to a lecture held in English language in London in 1854. Quoted here in Semper's original version. Eidgenössische Technische Hochschule in Zürich, Institut für Geschichte und Theorie der Architektur, Semper-Archiv, MS (124) 1.

[2] Otto Wagner, inaugural as professor at the Akademie der bildenden Künste in Wien, 1894. Quoted from Joseph August Lux, *Otto Wagner*, Munich, 1914, pp. 137 ff.

[3] Joseph August Lux, "Das Hotel, ein Bauproblem," *Der Architekt*, vol. XV (1909), pp. 17 ff. Here quoted from Otto Antonia Graf, *Die vergessene Wagnerschule*, Vienna and Munich, 1969 (*Schriften des Museums des 20. Jahrhunderts Wien*, vol. 3), p. 11.

[4] Josef Hoffmann, speech on Otto Wagner, 1910. First printed in *Jahrbuch der Gesellschaft österreichischer Architekten*, Vienna, 1910. Here quoted from *Finale und Auftakt – Wien 1898–1914. Literatur. Bildende Kunst. Musik*, edited by Otto Breicha and Gerhard Fritsch, Salzburg, 1964, pp. 216 ff.

[5] Otto Wagner, "Nachruf auf Joseph M. Olbrich," *Hohe Warte*, vol. IV (1908), no. 17. Here quoted from *Finale und Auftakt*, pp. 213 ff.

[6] Adolf Loos, "Aus meinem Leben," 1903. First printed in Adolf Loos, *Trotzdem*, Innsbruck, 1931. Here quoted from Adolf Loos, *Sämtliche Schriften in zwei Bänden*, edited by Franz Glück, vol. 1, Vienna and Munich, 1962, p. 252.

[7] Adolf Loos, "Ornament und Verbrechen," 1908. In *Trotzdem*. Here quoted from *Sämtliche Schriften*, vol. 1, pp. 276 ff.

[8] Adolf Loos, "Architektur," 1910. In *Trotzdem*. Here quoted from *Sämtliche Schriften*, vol. 1, pp. 302 ff.

[9] Adolf Loos, "Meine Bauschule," *Der Architekt*, vol. XIX (1913), no. 10, pp. 70, 71. Here quoted from *Sämtliche Werke*, vol. 1, pp. 322 ff.

[10] Josef Hoffmann, "Das Arbeitsprogramm der Wiener Werkstätte," *Hohe Warte*, vol. I (1904/05). Here quoted from *Finale und Auftakt*, pp. 209 ff.

[11] Hoffmann, ibid.